MW00471493

the truth always rises

Torches of Light for Life's Darker Passages

MOLLY McCORD, M.A.

* * *
SPIRITUALITY
UNIVERSITY
PRESS

ISBN: 978-0-9965680-5-0

Some chapters in this book were originally written in 2014 and formerly published in the ebook: *Guided By Your Light: Inspirations for Ridiculously Loving and Celebrating Yourself.*

www.ConsciousCoolChic.com

*This book is dedicated
to my amazing mom,
my favorite spiritual teacher
of all time.*

᱂

TABLE OF CONTENTS

INTRODUCTION 11

CARRYING TORCHES OF LIGHT 17

DECONDITIONING AND EGO DEATHS 23

TRUTH AS A MESSENGER OF POTENTIAL 33

FAITH IT 'TIL YOU MAKE IT 45

BLINDED BY THE LIGHT OF NEW TRUTHS...................... 51

THE JOURNEY OF KNOWING YOUR TRUTH 55

THE SOUL PURPOSE QUESTION 65

TRUTH AS A CHOICE POINT..................................... 73

SITTING WITH YOUR EMOTIONS 83

RETURN TO SENDER 91

THE OTHER FACES OF UNCONDITIONAL LOVE............. 95

OPENING UP TO GREATER COLLECTIVE ENERGY 105

EXPANDING YOUR ENERGY
    OUT INTO THE WORLD 111

WHEN BELIEVING IN YOUR TRUTH
    CARRIES YOU HIGHER 115

OWNING ALL OF YOUR ENERGY 135

THEN SOMETHING AMAZING
    HAPPENED AT A PARTY 145

YOUR TRUTH AS AN INNER FORTRESS........................... 153

REFERENCES AND RECOMMENDED RESOURCES 161

ABOUT MOLLY MCCORD..................................... 165

FREE CHAPTER EXCERPT....................................... 169

INTRODUCTION

I F TRUTH WERE A PHYSICAL element to you, would you envision it as a clear rippling stream, or a wild river roaring through steep canyon walls? Would you see truth as endless ocean waves continually flowing around the globe? Or maybe truth would appear as a quiet, remote lake resting in perfect tranquility.

Perhaps truth would be clean, pristine air; untouched areas of the troposhere, rising up to kiss the cosmos. Truth as pure as air that fills every single breath of every living being on the planet. Maybe this physical manifestation of truth glides and swirls, soars alongside clouds, clears tragic storms, and purifies what remains.

Or would you see truth as the hardiness of earth and the rising pride of mountains? Visible and everlasting, as it forms the deepest ocean trenches and the driest desert lands. Solid summits, flourishing valleys, and Grand Canyon gorges that have existed on the planet for billions of years. Truth that is steady, reliable, and timeless.

Or is truth a roaring fire that burns eternally, wildly, with a tireless passion for life? An energy scorching and blazing with fierce determination that sears through anything that stands in its way. A physical version of truth that burns brightly, flows steadily like lava, and tempers itself as needed to maintain its flames.

Truth could be any, or all, of these natural physical elements. Truth is one of those concepts—like gratitude, forgiveness, compassion, soul, and love—that carries a meaning we can feel and know energetically, while intellectually holding many explanations that fit its timeless form. Truth has long been explored, danced with, and defined by many masters, prophets, and spiritual leaders. We have searched for its understanding for centuries, seeking a deeper, more intimate knowingness of its essence. Numerous teachers have shared their understandings of truth, each attempting to capture a description of the indescribable:

Buddha said, "Three things cannot be long hidden: the sun, the moon, and the truth."

Krishna said, "Understanding immortality, those who are wise do not seek for truth among those things which are impermanent."

Jesus Christ said, "Wisdom is the seeking of truth, and anyone who seeks the truth will avoid the traps in life that destroy the spirit."

Gandhi practiced his understanding of truth by focusing on being in the world, without being of it. "When I despair, I remember that all through history the way of truth and love have always won. There have been tyrants and murderers, and for a time, they can seem invincible, but in the end, they always fall. Think of it--always."

Swami Vivekananda said, "All truth is eternal. Truth is nobody's property; no race, no individual can lay any exclusive claim to it. Truth is the nature of all souls."

In Zen Buddhism, the ability to have instant knowing is called *satori*, or *kensho*, which means "seeing into one's true nature." It is an immediate and clear connection to truth.

Ancient teachings and texts provide a solid basis on

the search for truth. In modern times, the seeking of truth, in all its plentiful forms, is alive and stronger than ever. The Merriam-Webster dictionary gives truth only four official explanations, but it easily could have pages of meanings from countless sources. Multiple understandings of truth can reside at once, expanding and widening the definition of a word that can be hard to grasp and fleeting to permanently hold. There is no single *truth*, but there are numerous truths that emerge from a central spoke in the wheel.

We can also file *truth* under a number of genres: Personal truths. Political truths. Historical truths. Physical truths. Spiritual truths. Your personal truth is based on your belief systems; as in, what you find meaningful, valuable, and of importance in life. Belief systems reflect where you find value and resonance in the world at large. You believe in certain ideals, politics, principles, rules, and personal understandings of yourself. You believe in what is possible for you in your life, or conversely, what is not possible because it is outside of your belief system. Truth may have evolving definitions based on your evolving personal experiences. If you look back on your life, you'll probably see how truth shifted to different meanings throughout your growth. At the age of 16, perhaps truth was tied to your desire for independence or freedom from your family. Maybe when you were 24 years old, truth was the desire to follow a career calling or start a family. Maybe when you were 33 years old, truth was related to your new sense of self and personal values. Maybe yesterday your truth was found in maintaining your calm during a heavily-charged political conversation.

In this book, we are exploring more about truth as it presents itself on the rocky, roller coaster path of spiritual awakening. Life forces us to descend into darker passages where we enter caves of despair and hallways of fear. We experience ego deaths, intense emotions, rejection, judgment, shame, or guilt. When we have been wronged or betrayed.... When we have experienced lies, deceit or manipulation... When we have held back a full story or have known that information is being hidden or covered up, we relentlessly navigate through the shadows, dark corners, and hidden secrets to return to the truth. As we experience untruth in our lives, we can choose to forge ahead with a deeper knowingness that at some point in time, perhaps later than the ego prefers, the real truth will be brought to the light.

Just as we descend into the dark, we always ascend back up into a place of higher truth and inner knowingness. For each fall, there is a rise. For each period of doubt, there is new wisdom to gain. Perhaps everything in the Universe, including the earth, water, fire, and air, are all ultimately making its way towards greater truth at all times. A grand experiment is underway in which we are invited and enticed to participate in the experience of truth as we move through the valleys, summits, and peaks of life. We discover the truth of what we believe, what matters the most, what holds value and meaning, what our feelings reveal, and the endless flame of inner truth that burns in the private pockets of our hearts.

There is no single definition of truth presented here, but you will find a common thread that I believe connects all understandings of the word: unconditional love. The hardest parts of our lives, those darkest of passages, are when we feel the most disconnected from a bigger love. We are often pushed down, down, down into the lowest parts of our being and experience very difficult situations.

The stories and messages in this book explore how challenging it can be to connect with a deeper truth of unconditional love, especially as we experience rejection, judgment, and the power of choice points. Truth shows up as you decondition from limiting beliefs, experience ego deaths, explore your soul purpose, and sit in the power of your feelings. Truth emerges on the rocky path of creative self-expression and believing in yourself while also connecting to huge amounts of faith. Relationships can be powerful messengers of truth as you return energy to the original sender, practice accepting those who do not see the real you, and honor the importance of owning all of your energy – talents, power, wisdom, and abilities – regardless of anyone else's actions or words.

Each of these areas of life contain the potential to amplify the truth of your feelings, what is in your heart, and what you believe is possible for yourself in this world. I hope you connect with reminders of what truth can look like, or perhaps just where you can leave an open window for it to climb in at the right time, perhaps even when you least expect it. Sometimes we have to play a "long game" with truth, meaning it does not show up to validate us immediately or reveal itself on an expected timeline. We have to stick it out, get stronger, stay open, and continue to trust.

If you are looking for more strength, faith, and trust in your life right about now, I sincerely hope this book delivers those messages to your heart, mind, and soul. The darker phases often challenge us deeply. But just as the lotus flower rises up through the mud, or how exquisite crystals grow in the most isolated of caves, we are always surrounded by truth as a natural presence on the planet. Truth grows and breathes, regardless of anything else that is happening externally. I hope you feel that strength and power within you, too, as the truth of who you are continues to rise.

CARRYING TORCHES OF LIGHT

CONSIDER THIS: THE BRAVEST SOULS are the ones who volunteered to go first with their light into the darkest of corners in their lives and out in the world. Your soul carries a torch of light for others to recognize, yet is not an easy path, nor for the egoically unstable, because many false parts of yourself will be dismantled along the way. There will be times when you have to dig within for more strength and fortitude.

As your soul carries this torch, high and mighty above the density of darkness, you are met with shadows, fears, and wounds with each careful step. This blazing light reveals where you are unhappy, unfulfilled, and perhaps lost. Rejection, abandonment, betrayal, or abuse has shined back at you in a glaring way; the pain danced with giant shadows on endless cave walls. You experienced harsh ego deaths or traumatic life losses as everything that once held meaning was scorched away, leaving burn marks and scars that healed slowly.

These were not the aspects of yourself you were hoping to find on a spiritual journey of truth.

Perhaps you thought holding and being the light meant something grand and majestic, yet you only felt more separation and despair. Maybe you started to believe that it was all a mistake, a wrong turn, a circular path in the dark that only led back to the same starting point of hopelessness again and again. Your aching arms grew heavy with the ceaseless weight of this torch. You faced deep fears of missing out on parts of your life and wondering why everything was so hard. So dang hard at times. You may have doubted yourself numerous times on your spiritual path. You may have looked back on your choices and felt a growing burden of regret.

And this is exactly why modern spiritual growth can be tricky. You may have been holding expectations that a spiritual path would make it all be easier; that you would manifest everything you wanted easily, quickly, and with huge joy. A lot of spiritual messages promote manufactured positivity and unrealistic expectations; the propaganda is rampant in spiritual circles. Surely life must be easier and more fulfilling now that you have tuned in to your spiritual self, so what are you doing wrong? Is it better for everyone else and you missed the bus somehow?

The truth is that a spiritual path can be harder at first because you are seeing everything in your life that is not working. Light separates away from anything that is not a true match for its vibration. In order to improve or fix something, you have to notice where it is broken and why you are not satisfied with it. The separation and pain that transpires is a revelation as you see where you want to grow personally, or change your relationships, or follow a dream, or completely change professions to do what you have always loved.

Part of your soul's growth during this time is understanding that you have always been doing the best you could at each period in your life. There were never any wrong turns, in truth, because that is not possible in this endless playground of energies. Every experience, relationship, choice, and behavior holds value from a spiritual perspective. Yet maybe you are now seeing where you gave your power to others or circumstances outside of your control. Light of a higher truth will reveal many unconscious aspects of yourself, including:

> • *Have you trained yourself to regularly look for validation from others?*
> • *Have you over-relied on others to determine your personal worth?*
> • *Have you been comparing your life to everyone else's to figure out if you're happy enough?*
> • *Have you been blaming yourself for what you have unconsciously created?*

All of these understandings point to new answers around your personal truth now. What feels right? What resonates strongly? What must shift within you so that you can step forward with this knowingness? The beauty of spiritual growth is that once you become aware of these parts of yourself, you grow with higher consciousness.

For example, when you feel exceptionally hard on yourself, notice that those messages come from your ego. The ego is the mental plane that is trying to find a way to fit into an expectation, control, feelings of power, unconscious programming, unhealthy childhood conditioning, or where you have tried to force your unique piece into the puzzle.

The ego is:

> • *looking for validation and acknowledgement externally.*
> • *trying to protect itself from experiencing the pain of solitude, abandonment, rejection, and hurt that it has*

known before.
* *focusing on how to belong or live up to expectations.*
* *trained to defend against being hurt.*
* *protecting itself from harm.*
* *seeking unconditional love.*

The unconditional love your ego seeks is found in your heart.

Your heart is:

* *a place of eternal safety that carries acceptance, acknowledgement, and love.*
* *does not allow other messages to enter its space and stay unless it is of the highest levels of love.*
* *a warm sanctuary of validation, acceptance, and happiness that beats wildly for your ongoing peace.*
* *simply welcomes all feelings as temporary visitors.*
* *encourages expression of fears so you can release them.*
* *a loving place of comfort and respite with no expectations.*

Your ego is looking for what your heart can provide, but due to constant external stimuli, you turn outward to seek that which resides internally. It is a game you play until you return to the energy of your heart that you always hold. When you master this game, you master your needs more fully. You master more of your spiritual path. You master your current truth because it lives in your heart as unconditional love. You master your personal truth.

When you get quiet within your heart, you will feel calm and reassured around your path. You will see that it is leading somewhere wonderful, even when you feel lost in the dark, but now you have the courage to keep going forward as you create exactly what you want. No one else can do it for you, so acknowledge that you are doing it now. Turn away from comparison and what you perceived as wrong. Instead, return to the wisdom of your heart as it cheers you forward on your spiritual path of greater self-love and understanding.

Torches of light hold up the truth in the darkest hours. Walking through the shadows is often the hardest aspect of the path, especially as you begin to decondition from old truths and experience ego deaths.

DECONDITIONING AND EGO DEATHS

WHAT WE UNDERSTAND AS A truth in our lives, consciously or unconsciously, is typically absorbed or programmed at an early age. We learn what is right or wrong in the world based on who influences our beliefs, which typically includes parents, siblings, and immediate family members. Family heritage, culture, politics, and belief systems all play a primary role in determining what we believe as truth in the world, as well as establishing our values. We explore the other options, understandings, or truths that also live and breathe in the world. This has become easier to research in recent decades as the internet and social media have opened us up to new belief systems and world views. Oftentimes, a discomfort or inner struggle emerges that is not ultimately satisfied with accepting what we previously held to be true. Noticing these changes is the beginning of a period of important inquiry.

On a spiritual awakening journey, we begin to question on a deeper level what is true for us individually. We question or challenge what we were taught, such as religious perspectives, political opinions, spiritual understandings, and/or belief systems.

Think of truth as what you eat off of your plate that sustains you and nourishes you. When you were younger, you probably ate what was served to you because it was the best option for your family, a classic recipe, affordable, or simply what was known. You ate it and accepted it as your dinner.

Then as you stepped away from your upbringing, you started to see more truths out in the world. Perhaps you read, traveled, questioned, and expanded your world views to see what was being served on other people's plates. Other recipes and specialty foods were introduced. Perhaps those exotic offerings piqued your interest or you felt a desire to sample new flavors. A favorite perception you've gnawed on for years now tastes bland. A previously accepted spiritual understanding feels like empty carbs. Truths you used to enjoy have become unfulfilling and leave you wanting more. Blah, yuck, meh, no thank you. Those tastes do not resonate anymore. Or you realize you're allergic to an ingredient. You are looking for a new truth that is more nourishing, satisfying, and loving of where you are now.

When you realize there is a lack of nutrition, you typically begin to seek more fulfilling sustenance, while also experience a deconditioning of what you previously claimed as a truth. Deconditioning from a truth is essentially when you say, nope, that doesn't work for me anymore. For example, you may discover that the belief systems you grew up practicing have gaping holes in how you now view and understand yourself, as well as the world at large. This deconditioning is often connected to an ego death, which is when we have put our self-identity into something we believed and identified with at an ego level.

We all have an ego. There are numerous spiritual teachings that discuss how to get rid of the ego, or do away with the ego. I disagree. We have an ego to form our individual identities and to support living the life that is best for us. The true problem is found between the healthy ego and the false, or unhealthy, ego.

A healthy ego gives you confidence, motivation, clarity, and the willingness to take risks. A healthy ego stems from a place of self-love and self-acceptance of who you are and what you want based on your internal self-definitions. A healthy ego enables you to live a satisfying life because you feel good claiming your talents, abilities, gifts, and self-expression. A healthy ego is connected to the desire to be stronger and more loving within self. A healthy ego amplifies inner power and self-confidence.

A false ego, or unhealthy ego, is the negative version of the ego that can get out of control. It can be competitive, materialistic, power-hungry, destructive, self-obsessed, self-absorbed, and overly focused on external satisfaction. A false ego does not have enough healthy nutrients within it. It wants to exert power, demonstrate superiority, control through money or status, dominate, destroy, and run the world – just to name a few possibilities. An unhealthy ego holds the intention to be something false out of a need to prove itself from ultimately a place of fear.

Deconditioning the false ego is essential to understand your truth. As more self-acceptance, self-love, and self-confidence rise within you, you will notice new choice points around your ego's energies. The false ego may push back out of fears to this new territory. The false ego will look to maintain control or resist change, but ultimately the new truth that is emerging within you will feel stronger. An ego death of the false ego is underway.

Ego deaths occur when the truth that was important to our false ego is stripped away. We are forced, nose to plate, to stare at a new understanding of how we have used our energy – and did it really serve up what we wanted? Ego deaths reveal where we held false or weak truths that do not support who we really are at the core of our being. We all hold truths around money, status, possessions, relationships, and identity masks. How much excessive power have you given those areas of your life? Is it satisfying all of you? Perhaps you became accustomed to eating a lot of fast food only to realize those choices were making you sick because they held no true love or real acceptance. Deconditioning removes these false layers of ego. Deconditioning removes false power.

Think of your ego as sugar. Some sugars are healthier, like those found in fruits, honey, beets, or sweet potatoes. Other sugars are very damaging, harmful and excessive, especially when consumed over a long period of time. Ego deaths remove the unhealthy aspects of yourself and your life that do not really sustain your long-term goals or inner world. The truth of who you are at the core of your being removes the excessive false ego that no longer feels healthy.

You can experience an ego death of who you were before a new self-identity or belief system is known. Emptiness may result as you clear off your plate and not know what to eat instead. A void is experienced. Then seeking begins as an exploration of different spiritual beliefs, practices, and understandings unfold.

When we start to decondition from previous truths and our ego releases its addiction to sugar, or false power, a beautiful opening occurs: you start to see more spiritual messengers in the world. You may feel a new willingness to learn or expand what you believe to be true. New spiritual teachers arrive to re-connect you with a healthier truth that fits your present state and needs.

A solid force of rising truth in my life has been my mom. She is one of my greatest spiritual teachers because of the comfort, peace, balance, and hope she has continually brought into my awareness during hard times. Whether I needed to call her from my college dorm room, or sit with her in the living room, both of us holding big cups of hot tea, or meet her for a two hour Sunday lunch, my mom has always known the right truth to set down on the table and offer me.

When I felt fear or anxiety around a loved one's choices, and I wanted to protect them from harm but felt hopeless, my mom wisely said, "God travels with everyone no matter where they are on their path." *Yes, yes, I could calm down my fears around their next steps.*

When I was in my late twenties, I thought that I "should" be getting married soon because that was a "typical" life event in one's twenties. The pressure to get married and have a family was increasing internally, yet I still felt wildly independent and up for a big adventure, like moving to Paris. My mom knowingly said, "There is good and bad with every life choice. There are good things that come with being married, and good things that come with being single. There are also hard things that come with marriage, such as no longer having the amount of independence you want right now. Everything has its pros and cons. Focus on the pros of right now and the benefits of being single." *Yes, yes, I could release my self-expectations with that understanding.*

When I was exhausted by crazy office dynamics, or there was stupid drama unfolding in my workplace, my mom's forty years of real world work experience could provide this perspective: "Anytime there is more than one person in a workplace, there will be conflict of some kind. People are always figuring something out with each other. Just remember what you want to bring to the conversation or to the table. That is where your power is."

Yes, yes, I could relax more knowing it was an ongoing dance of human relationships working themselves out.

When I was overly focused on whether or not a relationship was "the right one", she would bring me back to a balanced place by asking me to evaluate it based on all of the components of a healthy relationship: "The right person should connect with most of you, not just one part of who you are or one aspect of your life. They should know your seriousness and your silliness, and everything in between. A relationship is not one thing, it is multiple pieces of two people interacting and coming together." *Yes, yes, I could see what was connecting and what was lacking from a more clear-headed space.*

When I felt wounded by a person's hurtful words, my mom reminded me of the power of detachment and to practice being an observer, while not shutting down my heart. "It is okay to feel hurt and to allow those feelings to be heard. When someone is mean to us, we feel it. It hurts. But the other side of this, is that it really is not about you at all. Think of him as an It. Look at It. Look at what It is doing. Wow, It sure seems angry about something that has nothing to do with you." *Yes, yes, I could step back and see how their words and actions simply reflected how they moved in the world.*

I have carried these many messages of truth in my heart for years because each one strongly resonates with an inner level of comfort. Our spiritual teachers reconnect us with that internal place. They bring us back to balance, back to peace, and back to our own loving nature. They remind us of the truths we actively claim for ourselves, and show us where we have felt disconnected from higher wisdom. They recondition us to hold more love within ourselves.

It often takes time to make healthier decisions. We

have to continually practice and re-condition ourselves to see with new eyes, new perspectives. We can be unconsciously addicted to certain understandings that we have held for years, and it may be a challenge to integrate a new truth into our daily lives. Perhaps you could think of it as dropping excessive sugar from your diet. Take this story as an example.

A young mother in India was worried about her son who was addicted to sugar. He loved sugar in all forms, and was consuming too much of it on a daily basis. No matter what she tried to say, the mother could not get him to change his habits. She realized the only way to get her son to stop eating sugar was to hear the message directly from his idol, Gandhi.

The next day, the mother and her son set out on a long trek to visit Gandhi and ask for his help in changing his excessive eating habits. They found him in a village, and waited hours to meet with him. Finally, they arrived in front of the acclaimed spiritual teacher and the mother told Gandhi her situation.

"I wish for my son to stop eating so much sugar, but he won't listen to me. He is addicted to sugar and I am worried about his health and his weight. I hope he will listen to you, as you are his hero. Can you help me?"

Gandhi listened intently to her concerns. Then he replied, "Yes, I can help you. Please return here in three days with your son."

The mother, confused but willing, made the long walk back to her village with the promise of returning three days later to see Gandhi again.

After watching her son consume a lot of sugar for another three days, the mother was eager to return to the spiritual teacher for his guidance. On the morning of the third day, she woke up early with great anticipation. They made the trip back to his village and were granted early permission to sit with him.

Gandhi leaned forward and calmly said, "Please, young son, you must stop eating sugar. It is not good for you and your mother is worried. Will you please stop eating so much sugar every day?"

The boy nodded. He was mesmerized as his hero gave him this advice.

The young mother was grateful for the message, but also confused. "Thank you for guiding my son. I believe he now understands the issue after hearing it from you. But why did you not give him that simple advice when we visited you three days ago?"

Gandhi replied, "Because I was addicted to sugar myself three days ago."

We are all human beings in progress. Although removing sugar is literal in this story, it also highlights how deconditioning from our long-held habits takes time. Dropping sugar is deconditioning from expired truths. Dropping sugar is releasing unhealthy ego energies. New practices may take time to adjust to as you let go of who you have been in the world and start building up who you truly are after the false energies and addictive sugars are removed. Doing it in only three days wouldn't be so bad, either.

Every year, millions of trees release dead leaves that flutter and fall to the ground, dropping what is complete and what will not serve the tree's next cycle of growth come spring time. These leaves have fully matured and fulfilled their potential; now they are let loose to nourish the earth as mulch and debris. Deconditioning and ego deaths are the leaves of life. A single leaf grew in the sunshine and rain, providing nourishment as a temporary visitor of the tree's ongoing growth. We can take these natural cycles for granted and miss the wisdom of the process: for the tree to be stronger and stable, it must release what is temporary if it cannot be integrated as long-term truth.

The right truth for you will always speak to a bigger energy of love within yourself. Truth grows up to the highest parts in your energy field, opens the doors to that forgotten or neglected place, and asks for your loving attention. Just as we need to release and shed what does not serve our long-term growth, we need people in our lives who re-direct us back to unconditional love. Deconditioning is taking an active role in allowing your false ego and unhealthy truths to be released so you can create greater alignment between your healthy ego and a higher truth.

But what happens when the truth of who you are feels weak or underdeveloped within you?

⚘

TRUTH AS A MESSENGER OF POTENTIAL

M Y CAR'S ENGINE HUMMED IN the parking space stall. Windshield wipers swooshed the soft rain drops away every twenty seconds, revealing the descending darkness. Warm air from the heaters blasted onto my cheeks. I unhooked my seat belt and leaned over to grab my messenger bag in the passenger seat. I peered down inside and nervously shuffled the papers, perhaps for the fortieth time, just to move my anxious hands. The pile included an official query letter, an outline, chapter descriptions, the first few chapters, and a written summary. *Hope I'm not missing anything.*

Deep breath. *Okay, I can do this.*

I turned the car off and stepped outside into the cold rain, merciless and bitter. As I dashed to the library entrance, butterflies danced in my stomach as if they were in cahoots with the rainfall, the internal and the external creating puddles and nerves. *It is only a first impression and opening conversation.*

Through the doors, into the hushed hallway, courage moved up my body and confidence gathered in my head. *Maybe being at the library is a good omen.* I switched my messenger bag from the right to the left shoulder. *It will be fine no matter what.*

The meeting room was nearly at capacity. I took a seat in the back of the room, observing other hopeful writers and interested spectators. Then I calmly centered myself by staring straight ahead as the butterflies started to settle, retreat. The empty whiteboard at the front of the room glowed like a full moon. Once again I reviewed my quick pitch in my head just as I did numerous times on the drive over here; radio off, rain drops on.

For two years now I had tried to connect with a literary agent. All attempts had failed. Getting a literary agent's attention is no easy feat, as any writer looking to publish their first book could tell you. Rejections and "no thank you" replies were expected. At least those were a response of some kind. Even hearing you were the worst submission they ever saw would at least provide a smidge of feedback or closure to move on to the next agency. The silence of no response was even worse: did anyone even receive my query? Was it the right agent to reach out to? Did I even stand a chance, or was this a giant waste of time, a silly dream that only happens for a select few with the right connections?

I decided to change my strategy. Instead of reaching out to New York City literary offices, I was attempting to make a local connection in Seattle. This agent was important and influential because she represented authors with many books, big contracts, and movie deals. She knew the business and what books would sell. If I could get even a minute of her time to do a quick pitch, maybe I'd finally get somewhere with my author dream. The ongoing mental part of this publishing game was to put aside all previous rejections so I could be a clean slate, a positive mindset of new potential. *Every day is a new day.*

The literary agent walked in and put her bag on the

front table. Her rain coat hung from her arms as her textured red tunic swooshed above the desk, danced across the whiteboard full moon. The talking room quickly quieted down as we all fell into school children mode, not wanting to disturb the teacher or be the one who stood out for the wrong reasons. She began with a few welcoming remarks, casual pleasantries, and passed out her business cards. I counted thirty-one heads in the rows in front of me. Plus six people in my row. All people who were probably looking for her attention and approval; seeking her expertise and feedback. I had no idea so many would be here tonight, but then again, it shouldn't be a surprise. Millions of people dream about writing a book and being published.

The group's laughter brought me back to the moment. She was moving her hand through her short brown hair, absentmindedly, and talking about popular book sales so far for this year, 2009. The publishing industry was going strong. Publishers were looking for even more books to invest in. Backs became straighter in chairs, heads rose up higher. Hands went up.

Her talk lasted for nearly an hour. She answered questions about books and publishing and trends and favorite book covers. One person – *that* person in every crowd – went on and on about literary classics and why none were written these days. Her red tunic swayed further and further away from him.

After the official presentation ended, a small crowd formed around her with questions and inquiries and introductions. She asked some people to email her next week. She thanked others for attending. A select few even made her smile.

I waited in my seat, telling myself it was not fear that was keeping me glued here but the ability to be patient and trusting and to see what happened next. The reality of this next step suddenly felt very big and important now that a breakthrough was possible. Butterflies started spreading their wings, fluttering awake.

But as the talking heads dispersed, I knew I'd have to put myself in front of her. If this literary agent left the room, and I never spoke with her — never at least tried to present my work — would I hate myself for not making an attempt?

Yes.

I gathered together my papers, in case she was interested in anything I said, and stood up to get in front of her. She had been slowly making her way to the back of the room, stopping to answer questions about books becoming movies. At any moment she could just walk away and be done with the evening's events. I stood within talking distance, probably appearing a tad nervous as my right high heel softly twitched. The butterflies were making that foot dance.

Almost instantly, three people walked away from her, and then she turned in my direction, the new face in front of her. Her arms were crossed, glasses sliding down her nose. I had no time to breathe. The words just started spilling out.

"I am nearly done writing a travel memoir about my years of living in Paris that include adventure, love, trust, and how we keep growing with every realized dream. Is that a genre that you have any interest in?"

She lightly shrugged. "Oh, those books can be hit or miss. They are trendy now, but not likely to last so my ability to represent them depends on a number of things. Where would it be in a bookstore?"

I knew the answer to that question after talking with a bookstore owner. "It would be in the travel section, or perhaps the self-help area, depending on the reviewers."

Her eyes peered over the top of her glasses. "But now you're back here in Seattle, you're not in Paris?"

"Right, because the story turns from the external adventure to an internal exploration of what we carry inside-"

"People don't want sad stories about failed dreams."

My face started frowning, stuttering, confused. "That-that isn't the message at all. It is about how our dreams keep going and change forms and -"

My trepidation had now changed to annoyance, so I quickly shifted focus. "And I also wrote a guidebook on Paris because I thought it could be a companion to the travel memoir. An easy cross-sell between the books -"

She raised her eyebrows at me and tilted her head with a slight frown, since surely I did not have the authority to write a guidebook on Paris. Then without another word, she turned and walked back to the front of the room.

What a bitch. I grabbed my bag off the floor briskly, more embarrassed than insulted. I had very low expectations for tonight, but even those ground-level hopes proved to be too high. Perhaps I could have explained my books better if I wasn't so nervous, or she wasn't the right person for my genre, or she was incredibly tired and worn out on this dark Thursday night.

Or maybe she was right. Maybe the travel memoir genre was over and done; a mere trend that had served its time and was no longer of interest to readers. What did I know about selling books or how the business side of publishing worked? Maybe I could not pull off selling a guidebook to Paris if I did not possess the necessary authority, no matter how intimately I knew the city. If she was so well connected and experienced, then it would be smart of me to at least listen to her non-interest in my books – right?

I walked back to the car, welcoming the rain drops on my head and feeling that the library was now the worst place to be. My butterflies had left the building as a heaviness of defeat rose up in my heart, mind, dreams. I quietly knew I was not very strong in my creative self. I felt hopeful, but also insecure; willing to try anything, yet not internally strong enough to rely on my own self-validation. The ongoing rejection was normal for writers; yes, yes, yes. But if so many people before me had found a way to get published, surely there was a place on the bookshelf for one more contribution. Unless the discouragement and rejection took me out first.

Most days, I am a dedicated writer and artist; focused and working away with my oh-so-happy hands. Most days, I feel inspired and have confidence in my work. Most days, I feel pretty darn good about the creative experience. Most days, I am on a roll.

Then there are the other days.

The days where I feel like I am not doing enough. The days where I find myself at a library staring down the rows of books, wondering if my writing is good enough. The days where I get too stuck in my head and feel like I should be better

On those days, my head gets spinning in creative fear and it can be hard to jump off that merry-go-round. My energy plummets down, down, down, as if sinking to the ocean floor.

What do I have to offer that is different and new? Are "they" more talented, creative, recognized, and special than I? Are "they" more qualified to write with more incredibly brilliant things to say?

These thoughts mean one thing: I need to get out of

the house to get out of my head. I look for anything that alleviates the ego's hypersensitivity tends to do the trick: exercising, grabbing a cup of tea, reading a book, and sitting in a park are all great remedies. But there is one place in particular where I love to go to turn-off my ego: IKEA.

I just need to get out of my head and get into IKEA.

I am in love with IKEA. Why? Because strolling through the giant store is an immediate spark for the visual senses. The colors, shapes, textures, and layouts relax me for some odd reason. Just following the winding path through the store is calming because I don't have to do anything except enjoy the staged rooms and end cap displays and geometrically-pleasing shapes of everything. If only life were as calm and trustworthy as an IKEA walkway. And I like to believe that IKEA is in love with me, too, because of how often I invest quality time in our blue-and-yellow relationship. If they offered personally monogrammed shopping bags to celebrate our courtship, mine would travel with me everywhere.

With my heart leading the way, my ego is turned down and does nothing except marvel at the efficiency of Swedish engineering and the most difficult words in the world to pronounce. My cart fills up with colorful napkins, a must-have throw pillow, storage boxes for tea bags, a cute Christmas decoration on "Last Call" special because it's February, and more wine glasses that we don't really need. This lazy parade and all of these goodies have taken me out of being my own worst enemy, a.k.a. my ego's fears. I leave my silly creative fears in the car—along with the reusable shopping bags—and allow myself to simply *be* in this experience.

The cart tinkers and clinks along the guided pathway until I stop in the warmth of the lighting section. Dang, this area is *bright*. Hundreds of light fixtures adorn every surface and direction. Tall skinny lamps, round table lamps, thin wall sconces, handy portable lights. Designs exist for fancy living room, casual bedrooms, playful kids spaces, and funky random rooms. Each one offers a different vibrancy, size, and function, yet there's room for all of them to shine their full wattage.

Standing here, I feel the warmth on my fingers, arms, cheeks. The beauty of light is that we seek it out through other sources instinctively, perhaps even intuitively. We gravitate towards it, indulge in it. I make my way through each display light, toying with its features and buttons.

Press on. Press off.

I loiter in the middle of all these fixtures as some illuminating thoughts about dealing with creative fears pass through my mind. Why do we even compare ourselves to other people's talents or achievements? It is such a self-defeating process to begin with because it means no one is truly seen for who they are or what they offer; they are simply held up against another for evaluation.

Do I even want to live that way? No.

Click off.

Does anyone really want to live that way? No.

Click on.

So what is going on underneath the surface, and what can I do to change that? As I stroll through the aisles, I get to deeper truths around creative fears.

1. Recognize specifically what is triggering the comparison. What is the fear that is being stimulated: the desire to be seen and acknowledged? The fear of not being valued? The fear of not being good enough?

Let that vulnerable part surface and be seen. Allow it to be heard. Bring it to the light.

2. Send that vulnerable part high-wattage love, big hugs, and warm understanding. Send the ego confirmation that comparing is part of human nature at times. We are social beings who want to see where we fit into the social fabric around us. Take the comparison simply as a "checking in point" for what is possible in the world. Use the vulnerability as a place of inspiration. Send it more high-wattage love.

3. Compare and despair? It rhymes, so it's an easy adage to remember, but it's not a productive thought. That downward spiral can become one fast-moving slide, so I replace those two words with this rhyming pair: Admire and Inspire.
The best of others can bring out the best in us. What a gift to have so many people to find inspiration from! What a blessing to feel creative energy from others! How wonderful to feel the warmth of others' light! Allow the radiance of others to light a bigger path for all.

4. Everyone has two hands and one mind they can use to create, but we are each blessed with a unique creative voice from our individual souls. Never doubt the power of what we are each compelled to offer — it can never be duplicated.
Your soul essence has a light that is yours to broadcast and share. No one else can share your soul's creative voice in the world. Your soul only knows your personal truth and can only steer you in that direction.

5. What you are called to do in your heart is what you are called to do for the hearts of others. Claiming your soul's gifts without expectation, judgment or attachment is the primary commitment to your truth. You lose nothing and gain everything by shining your light brightly.

There is room for all of the many lights in the world to shine brightly and boldly.

Ahhhh. These are exactly the reminders the ego needs when it starts to act silly and slip down that rabbit hole of fear. I now feel so relaxed and calm after standing here with my heart light blazing. All credit goes to IKEA's lighting products.

Apparently, though, you're not supposed to stand with your eyes closed in the middle of the lighting section. I've been asked numerous times if I need help or have a problem with something. I smile and respond with an overly cheerful, "Oh no, I am GREAT!"

Turns out, that type of enthusiasm scares employees away. I gathered myself together and returned to the flowing concrete pathways, pushing the teetering cart that is now packed with decorative lanterns and a gorgeous serving platter.

I see so much clearer now how the world needs as many lights as possible to shine. Every light is valuable, seen, and special. Every light brings unique energy beyond what can be measured. Every light is a gift to and from the soul.

I believe it is the reason why we are all here: To shine boldly from the heart light that is waiting for us to turn — and leave — it on.

I purchased all of my must-have items, which have

increased in quantity even more after walking through the outdoor patio section. New seat cushions are a must for summer, after all. There is one problem with thinking so positively in IKEA: the yellow bags sure do get heavy.

As I load up my car and leave the parking garage, I have one more thought about the enlightening lighting department. It is silly, but it makes me happy.

I have this visual that every night, each light is turned off one by one to go to sleep…errr, save energy. As a single light is flicked off, all of the other lights say, "Thank you for adding so much warmth and beauty to the room today! It was perfect! See you tomorrow for another day of light!"

Then another light is turned off, and all the other lights say, "Thank you for doing your best today! We saw it and we recognize you! See you tomorrow for another day of light!"

Then another is light turned off, and all the lights say, "You were so amazing! We were so happy to be in your glow today! See you tomorrow for another day of light!"

And on and on it goes until every light is asleep. Then they are each turned back on tomorrow with fresh energy, strength and willingness to shine even more brightly.

Maybe publishing a book could happen for me. I have no idea how the pieces will come together, but if I really want it, I must persevere with greater amounts of trust and drop the doubt off in the trash.

When doubt shows up, it is a messenger of your temporary truth that is based in fear. Yet even this feeling can make you stronger because it can redirect you back to what is true for you. In order for a tree to grow UP it must first have stable roots that grow DOWN. Imagine pushing the doubt down into the earth and watching it morph into stronger faith. These roots ground and stabilize you for growth, as well as for the storms of life. Hearty, solid roots of faith will embed you to a bigger dream, even when you have no idea how it can possibly emerge in the real world yet.

~

FAITH IT 'TIL YOU MAKE IT

IN THE LATE 1890s, A woman named Florence Scovel was a children's illustrator for magazines, periodicals, and papers. She was a pioneer in this profession since women did not typically work outside of the home, much less attend school and find employment in their chosen field. Florence married another artist, Edwin Shinn, whom she met in college. Together, they were a part of the Ashcan School of Art, which was a group of artists that depicted realistic daily New York City life through the experiences of immigrants, workers, and street scenes. Florence's observations as an artist put her in greater touch with everyday peoples' lives.

Florence became a student of metaphysics in the early 1900's. She was inspired by New Thought spiritual teachings that had helped her develop more faith and focus on positive thoughts through the years. Eventually Florence felt compelled to write a book about what she had learned called *The Game of Life and How To Play It*. Her spiritual philosophy focused on the power of our thoughts, as well as incorporating messages from the Bible, with an emphasis on positive affirmations. Florence believed she could spread these messages to more working class people who were disenfranchised, turned off by other spiritual teachers, or who were not connected with a formal church.

Florence completed her book and sent it away for submission, but no traditional publisher would accept her manuscript. Undeterred, Florence held on to her belief in positive thinking and possibilities, as well as believing that her writing could provide hope and inspiration to many.

In 1925, Florence Scovel Shinn was one of the earliest women to self-publish her first book, *The Game of Life and How To Play It*.

Florence became a spiritual counselor and speaker, taking her messages to everyday people who needed a bit more hope and a little more faith. Her style was friendly, practical, and relatable in a manner that set her apart from other spiritual teachers. She eventually self-published two more books, *Your Word Is Your Wand* in 1928, and *The Secret Door To Success* in 1940. Her pioneering ways broke the mold of what was possible for women and authors, as well as expanded the New Thought Movement out to more societal circles.

History holds many stories of an individual who is marginalized, rejected, or denied access to resources who still persists toward their bigger dream. Florence Scovel Shinn is just one example of faith in herself, her messages, and her work in the world as something grander than one person. That bigger faith moved her forward.

Holding a bigger dream in your life can be encouraging, motivating, and inspiring. You may have dreams that originated in childhood, or something that came to mind just last week that is calling to you on a deeper level. It may be a dream that seems tangible and possible, or wildly unrealistic but fun to daydream about over your latest pour of red wine. You can get caught up in the possibilities and potentials, yet do not see how the dream can come together. Maybe the path does not feel clear, or the ground underneath your feet is shaky, or only the idea exists but you have no clarity around how to create the form. For whatever reasons, that big "something" is not unfolding. It is living and breathing in your heart, but not yet within your grasp.

An energy inside you knows the dream is possible. You KNOW IT. (*you know it.*)

We have all heard the age-old adage "fake it 'til you make it". It is the idea that if you pretend to do something, you will eventually develop the skills, smarts, success, and confidence to pull it off with the validation of being "real". But let's slam on the brakes for a second because "pretend" has a low-vibrating energy. It has the undercoating of doubt, lack, and being revealed for a sham. The last thing your big dream would be is a sham. It does not even come close to having the energy of fake – *at all.* Anything fake is, by definition, the opposite of truth.

Your dreams and what you are creating for yourself are part of your inner truth. As a result, they deserve the best five-star, top-of-the-line, platinum *everything.* So let's upgrade this "faking it" philosophy. The good news is that anything of a lower energy can be turned into a higher expression with your focused intentions and commitment to a new level of trust. I propose upgrading from fake to faith. As in: Faith It 'Til You Make It.

Your definition of faith can be whatever fits you best: daily prayers, visiting your church, a spiritual practice, a special jewelry reminder, or a beautiful candle sitting on your desk that burns the sweetest scent – and you call it faith. The "what" is not important; it is the connection and belief in it that matters most. Faith is something that cannot be faked, not even to the smallest millimeter of doubt. Faith is huge, evolving, personal, and cosmic, surrounding you with a divine presence at all times. Faith will step in and replace anything "fake" with a higher intentional energy.

What does faith look like in the Real World? It comes out in these ways:

• How you speak to yourself about your goals. In private moments, do you tell yourself you can do this/have this/create this? Validate your dreams regularly and remind yourself that you are capable of so much more from yourself than you have known before. Of course you can do this/have this/create this. Of course.

• How you speak to others about your abilities and dreams. Often we can hold back our desires and wants out of a fear of sounding overly-confident or arrogant. People who love you want the best for you and want you to have everything in your heart.

On that note:

• Be selective about whom you share your dreams with to keep your faith alive and sacred. You do not owe everyone an explanation or reason for your dreams. Heck, you do not owe *anyone* an explanation or reason. But we all need cheerleaders and a support system, so choose wisely and honor yourself in the process.

• Trust that if something is not happening (or gets cancelled, or delayed, or falls apart) it is because something BETTER is on the way to you. Faith knows that not only is the glass *always* full, but it runneth over, darlin'. Keep the faith that everything around you is Divine and rejection is God's protection.

• Choose to believe in what is possible instead of what is visible. Eyesight is sooo overrated with faith because anything and everything can happen at any time. Anywhere. Miracles occur overnight and an unexpected new friend may hold the next steps of your dream. It can happen in the most amazing ways. Allow the opportunities to show up.

• Follow your gut. Your internal navigation system is your gut and it is powered by trust and faith. Amp it up! Dedicate time every day to following your gut in some way: reach out to a friend who keeps popping into your head, talk to someone new at a store, branch out in your social media networks, sign-up for a new class. Faith can walk in the door anywhere and be anyone.

Everything begins in energetic form, such as thoughts, dreams, or visions, before it takes shape in material form. Infuse your life with a higher level of faith and make a commitment to stick to it even when you cannot see anything happening.

Just as a tree is developing strong roots in the earth, a lot can be going on internally and under the surface. The ability to form a stable foundation of faith will ground you into what you are growing. Over time, the first stem pops up through the dirt. Then with its stable roots, the stem can sprout higher and grow its necessary branches. Those branches provide sustenance for the leaves to start budding. And all of this is happening on the faith that the sun's rays and drops of water will arrive to nourish the growth process.

We all have limitations and conditions in life we must work around. We can feel challenged to persist with faith in what we cannot see yet. Florence Scovel Shinn pioneered a new approach to sharing her teachings, regardless of rejection and going off the traditional path. Know that what seems intangible and improbable to our human minds does not exist in God/Spirit/Source energy. Spiritual energy is unlimited with options and potentials; anything can transpire as we take the dream forward one step at a time.

Reminders of faith can be found anywhere. With this renewed energy, I vow to keep carrying the possibility of writing a book, even though I do not know how it will happen or when it could be reality. If I am called to follow this path, I have faith that it is for a reason.

Faith is your opportunity to consciously root yourself into a dream that is calling you forward. Faith provides the foundation to help you withstand the challenges ahead, as well as to ensure you keep sprouting up to more of your own light.

ॐ

BLINDED BY THE LIGHT
OF NEW TRUTHS

D URING TIMES OF CHALLENGE AND struggle, it is easy to want to step back into what is known. To find the places of comfort, the darker corners of stability, the safe places of retreat. What is ahead can seem literally blinding: unknown and scary. Is it safe to go forward? Is there ground beneath my feet, just mere inches ahead? Why would I want to chance it if I am wrong?

The reason why we want to chance anything that calls to us is because it is actually the safest time to do so. Right now is a time of big choice points and letting go of those scaredy-cat versions of ourselves. Trusting and moving blindly ahead is incredibly supported because you are truly ready to be more stable in yourself than ever before.

If instead of turning from the light, you focus on turning towards it, you will start to feel the heat and hope and happiness that is surrounding you. You will see that the light is not actually blinding — it is warming. Warming and thawing you to your core, your talents, and your purpose. The heat and light are actually magnets that are pulling you forward and not wanting you to turn away. You are being asked to look at where you have traveled in recent years and to acknowledge how far you have come. Then hold that same evidence and truth for the new paths you are embarking upon. You will always have more than you need, and you will always find abundance in whatever you focus on. Would you <u>really</u> be led astray? Would you <u>really</u> be set up for something you could not handle? Would you <u>really</u> be pushed to grow and flourish and sprout new branches if you did not already have the foundation to hold them?

God/The Universe/Spirit/Source (whatever term is comfortable for you) trusts us to <u>only</u> grow in the directions that are best for ourselves. We are <u>only</u> being led to what is the natural next step, and to accepting that anything that is dying or passing has simply lived its purpose for us right now.

Butterflies instinctively feel the safest time to shed their cocoons during the light. The heat makes the transition easier, swifter, more comforting, more rewarding. Light evaporates darkness. The comfort of the cocoon gives way to the comfort of heat. The smaller home explodes into a world of unlimited potential and possibility that could not be seen in the intimate cocoon. How could we possibly want to deny the joy that comes from a greater comfort? How could we possibly want to turn away from a light that only encourages us to grow brighter, taller, stronger?

Instinctively, we don't want to truly turn away. We want to warm ourselves and go towards the heat that is not really meant to blind us. It is awakening us at a deep level that has never been tapped before. Now is the time to see transitions as holders of future joy. Now is the time to breathe in the sunlight deeply. Now is the time to release... let go...and trust that we have something more magnetically pulling us forward. And the blinding light will not deter that goodness from approaching.

What is ahead of us can feel unknown and undefined; we cannot yet see it clearly and it feels a bit scary. It can be too hard to look at The Future, and much easier to turn our heads away for the feel of comfort and safety The Past.

New emotional layers are being revealed as egos are shed and the vulnerable new skin that lies beneath is being brought to the surface. Relationships are shifting as a result of these layers being exfoliated, and we may be surprised by what lies beneath. Old friends and familiar relationships may take on a new assignment in a different direction or unexpected purpose in our lives. Issues that we thought we had put to bed are rising up again to be examined. It can be a time of rawness as new parts of ourselves are being exposed to the light; new parts that have never seen or felt this type of intensity.

Deconditioning and ego deaths shake up, loosen, and bring to the surface more messages to support our choice points so we can keep the good stuff and let go of the rest. The pieces, debris, and crumbs are floating all around us, like living in a snow globe. Swirling and spiraling, the transitions are everywhere and it can feel at times like nothing has landed just yet. Old behaviors and mindsets are becoming outdated, and some have become very obvious if we are aware of our own patterns and personal fears. Cocoons are being shed. Perhaps you'll notice more butterflies in the summer air. Perhaps you are feeling the tightness of your own cocoon? A new journey of knowing yourself more is underway.

THE JOURNEY OF
KNOWING YOUR TRUTH

THE ONLY PERSON WHO CAN truly know you is You. You are deep, wide, and vast; a brilliant combination of matter and light taking shape in this human definition. Take a moment right now to breathe in deeply and feel the expansion of your lungs, the air in your throat, the rise in your chest, the fullness of your diaphragm. When you focus on the simple wonders in the present moment, you shift into a new sense of presence about yourself that is filled with spectacular joy. Every breath is a journey into knowing yourself more. Every exhale is an expansion of your energy out into the world.

Take a moment right now to place your right hand on your heart and feel the pulse of your soul in your palm. Close your eyes and dip into the sensation. Your heart is a magnificent machine of soul-driven power. Your heart keeps you in your physical self because it loves you beyond measure and wants you to physically feel how much you are loved, in the palm of your hand. You are the only one who can know this soul-love about yourself; a direct physical link is created between your soul's vibration and the depths of your energy signature.

Knowing your truth is an endless journey into your inner light, brilliance, and vastness. The human experience is filled with new doors continually opening into your own energy. Throughout your life, you will be given endless opportunities to know yourself in new ways and to love yourself more in every situation. Anytime you need a blast of light, simply put your hand on your heart, breathe, and step into the energy of your self-love by visualizing it. This is your instant connection to your soul energy, available any time of the day and night, all weekends — and especially during holidays with family.

Hold the intention to love yourself and what is true for you no matter how imperfect life will be at times. You may search for perfection in people, words, ideas, experiences, and coffee makers, but you will probably find that your definition of "perfect" will evolve as you evolve. Instead of looking outside of yourself, consider this truth: Self-love is the only display of perfection in the Universe because it is unconditional love.

When you practice loving yourself, you are exuding perfection. You are holding the vibration of your truth in an honorable, joyful manner. You are tapping into the truth of yourself and diving deeper into the innate perfection of your timeless energy. Perfection is an inner experience of Self that is always with you internally and never obtainable externally. When you shift from focusing on perfection in the outer world, and instead honor the perfection in your inner world, you have raised your vibration to a ridiculously higher level.

And related to this, you – and you alone — are responsible for holding the highest possible opinion of yourself as you choose. You energetically set the tone for your self-love energy and others respond to this vibration, often unconsciously and unintentionally. You are a magnet for the love vibration that comes from honoring your needs, gifts, and deepest self. From this energy, you can call in any relationship, situation, or experience you desire. You are the magnet that attracts equal vibrations. When you are grounded in the essence of your self-love, you will begin to experience a completely new part of yourself in the external world as this energy is reflected back to you in unlimited ways.

You are gifted with exploring yourself as a dynamic being of unlimited potential and expansive dreams. How will you choose to direct the journey of knowing yourself? How will you choose to demonstrate this love responsibly and joyfully?

Many spiritual seekers will reach out to psychics, intuitive, energy healers, and other guides for insights about themselves. Talented individuals will give you empowering information that will resonate with your heart, and in turn, it will greatly assist your path. All spiritual guides are fulfilling a soul mission with their spiritual gifts to be of service to humanity's evolution and growth at this pivotal time. Yet regardless of how many sessions, readings, or healings you receive, return to your inner voice for guidance. Return to you. Trust what you feel about the information. Question what doesn't sit well with you. Notice where your energy rises or sinks. Do not give your power away. As you proceed on the journey of knowing your energy better, you will always know the best answers for what you need. The journey of this lifetime includes discovering your light on your terms.

There is no more sitting on the sidelines in the world of self-help as another tells you to love yourself. You must practice it regularly and on your own terms. You are living in a highly active time frame of self-discovery that requires your whole-hearted participation. You are in charge of yourself in all ways—mentally, emotionally, physically, energetically, financially, spiritually—and you are supported in expanding into your light essence even more. The world is requiring millions to step into their self-love state with devotion and presence. Together, we are all leading the way into new dream-filled experiences we have been waiting lifetimes to have.

The time is now. Are you mentally and emotionally ready to receive your dreams? Are you open to ease, grace, and peace? Are you curious what your path may be? Are you ready to venture forth with trust, faith, and happiness?

You have access to more knowledge, resources, and people than ever before in human history. The possibilities and potentials for your growth are unlimited. You have the capacity to shift, and shape, and turn your journey in any direction you choose.

Millions of souls are alive at this time to bring in awakening energies, consciousness expansion, and light-infused intentions. Never before has humanity experienced such a plethora of powerful, love-based energies on the planet. More and more people are becoming curious about their spiritual gifts, talents, and healing abilities. Thousands are awakening to their spiritual nature and seeking understanding to their life purpose. Amongst the turbulence, wars, feuds, fights, and fears, there is a huge anchoring of peace and love. A higher celebration is unfolding.

With the continual incoming waves of light and love, there is greater opportunity than ever to expand into all of You. It is a time to heal, release, transmute, reform, evolve, and expand into your full love vibration. You are highly revered and adored for being an intricate part of the human family as it undergoes significant transformational shifts. As you open up and welcome the opportunities for greater self-knowingness, you will feel a change in your personal energy field that is hard to describe. In fact, you won't be able to describe it because it is energy beyond words; it is your natural state. It is the vibration of light

Earth has been on a long journey filled with multiple energies. Through ongoing eras of grand transformations, the planet has experienced intense changes from pure light to hard darkness. Human evolution has known the simplicity of living with nature, to the harshness of the Dark Ages. Earth has ascended and descended in previous cycles of consciousness. Now there is a rising up of light as we collectively raise the globe up to a higher levels of love than it has ever known before. With the increase, there will be reactions from energies that do not wish to experience higher levels of peace, harmony, and cooperation because they will no longer be an energetic fit in this new paradigm. Light is leading the way, and even when the pushback from darker places is strong, you must carry forward with strength in yourself as a vessel of more love. You have the ability to be loving everywhere you are. The intention to *shine forth* and *love forward* will be exponentially fortified with your relentless focus on love.

Infuse everything you do on a daily basis with the intention of love. From your morning coffee, to stressful conversations, to boring chores, to your final thoughts before sleep, simply state that you exist in the continual energy of love and you feel celebrated by the Universe now.

The unconditional love vibration never leaves you, but you may lose your connection to it at times. It is okay when this happens. Do not punish yourself for forgetting to practice Self-love. Life responsibilities and your inner world will flood in stronger at times, and then eventually those circumstances will ebb out. Returning to unconditional love will happen more easily as you include it as a daily ritual in your life. As you lift up your morning coffee, declare that you love yourself. Easy as that to declare a personal truth.

How would you describe your unconditional love energy: Bright and sparkling? Light and swift? Wild and free? What color is it? Do you feel a texture or pattern around it? What does your Self-love essence look like in your mind's eye? Take a deep breath and sit in this feeling.

When you are ready, claim this energetic experience as your Self-love vibration. It will instantly open you up to greater Universal flows of joy, happiness, peace, forgiveness, and abundance. It is yours to play with and appreciate; to own and mold as you see fit.

When you give greater energetic intention and focus to this frequency, you will feel yourself evolving and expanding in new ways. You will naturally feel a celebration of yourself simply for being you: for being your energy, for living your story, for loving your gifts. You will feel an inner calm and quiet peace. You are opening up to your own light expression and living in it; living from it. It begins with your focused intention to recognize your unique vibration of love, and then committing to its connection regularly. Life will continue to flow, rush, and move around you at various speeds. Energies from all directions will be alive and interacting with you from the external world. But as you focus on feeling into your love vibration, you will develop a tougher barrier to external events; these energies will no longer intrude inside your safe, sacred place because it is already flooded with unconditional love. There is no room for anything else when your vessel is filled to the brim with the energy of your choosing.

Practice taking care of your energy field daily by focusing on unconditional love. Even if it is only two minutes in the car after school, or for thirty seconds as you heat up tea in the microwave, just breathe into the energy you feel. The more you engage in this practice, the more you will feel like You. Amplify this connection and you will experience your light. It is truly this simple to be guided by your light as you love yourself more. This is a clear truth to integrate.

As you ascend to greater strength in your personal truth, your awareness increases in numerous ways. You see how very powerful you are with your intentions, thoughts, beliefs, and actions. You notice your spiritual power lining up and coming together in incredible ways. You see how your intuition and instincts kick in faster, and that you can tune into energies with new consciousness.

As you raise your vibration, you also raise your responsibility. You raise your understanding around the ramifications and energetic consequences of what you choose and what you do. You see how your actions create reactions and ripple effects, some even lasting well into the future and into other timelines.

Part of spiritual mastery is understanding that you carry new levels of responsibility to honor now. Just as we mature from children to adults, we mature from spiritual children to spiritual adults who understand the bigger perspectives of the Universe. We see how we must be more intentional than ever, and act with full ownership of ourselves in all ways.

Of course, we *know* this, but that pesky ego can show up to the party and a fear can creep in the back door unexpectedly. These are exactly the times when we have to kick it up a notch with responsibility, ownership, and personal consciousness.

Own your spiritual power with greater spiritual responsibility that supports your mastery:

- Give yourself time to sit with a decision or choice.
- Discern what connects with your new energy, opposed to what is the "old way" of doing something.
- Get clear about your intentions before proceeding.
- Connect with your spiritual adult soul self who understands that you are always powerful and always in control of your energy.
- Ask: What is the most conscious choice I can make for everyone's highest and best good in this situation?

Think of a flowing river as it rolls along, following the rifts in the earth and winding around massive boulders. The water collects debris as it roars forward, and may get clogged in places, but it keeps moving with natural forces that cannot be stopped. The bends, curves, and waterfalls all create a wild ride; energy in continuous motion. The river's truth is mastery of the environment; the ability to both expand with increasing flow and to narrow through tighter passages. Water that is flowing with force, yet gentle enough to glide. This is mastery of its natural truth.

This journey allows you to embrace joy while also embracing the mastery of energies that you are here to experience. There may be harder, wiser choices to make at times, but they will also lead you to more perfect developments and outcomes because you are owning your spiritual power with more spiritual responsibility.

As you do this, the most driving question that typically emerges pertains to your soul purpose.

THE SOUL PURPOSE QUESTION

YOUR SOUL HAS BEEN ON a very long journey. Your soul has traveled dimensions, timelines, and channels of light to experience the fullness of a human adventure. You are a conglomeration of star sprinkles and light waves compressed into a physical body that is alive with a story longer than time. You are timeless.

And yet you are here. On earth with feet and hands and hair and an inquisitive mind. You feel an urge to question, explore, seek, and understand. You wish to discover your purpose, your reason for being. You feel led to understand your soul more, which is such a human frame of mind because how do you understand that which is unexplainable in words? Your soul is a dynamic energy field of light, sound, and even higher vibrations that do not register on the energetic Richter scale.

The Soul Purpose Question is typically asked because it holds great expectations and weight: "If I know my soul purpose, I will know everything I need to do in my life." The Soul Purpose Question is a big one, yet it has a very simple answer: You are alive to upgrade all areas of your life to the vibration of unconditional love.

Your soul is in human form to heal all energies back to their original source of love. You are present to love yourself daily as you learn, heal, and evolve through a myriad of circumstances. You are here to find the love in every part of yourself, in every person, in everything you encounter and touch. And yet—this is so much easier said than done.

Being human is an imperfect journey composed of multiple experiences that will feel like the *opposite* of love. You will have times of withholding love from those who hurt you; you will judge others for their actions or words. You will have endings, completions, and rough patches with people. You will perceive your power being challenged by another, or come up against deep inner emotions. You will have difficult conversations, intense reactions, and deep transformations along the way. Your perception and unconscious programming will tell you there is no love here; there is no love for this person and what they did to you, or said, or the actions they chose. Withholding love will feel more powerful than giving love.

When you take a step back and look with fresh eyes, you will see how this is absolutely perfect. You are being given an opportunity to elevate emotions UP to love. You are ascending your energy UP to light. You are identifying where there is a lack of love and releasing older versions of energy in order to experience Love from a higher viewpoint. You are transmuting fear into love. On a random Wednesday or a quiet Sunday.

Since unconditional love is the only perfection in the Universe, you are performing this task beautifully when you love, honor, and respect yourself. You are right on time and doing it perfectly as you find the love within yourself first, and act from that energetic space.

Your soul purpose is to work diligently to love your fears, your emotions, your ego, your "enemies," and your "imperfections" more. Apply tons of love to everything;

repeat every morning.

Your soul purpose is a love mission. Each person on the planet arrives with certain tasks to complete and energies to work with in order to accomplish their love mission. To be successful, you require certain life attributes that will trigger you to grow:

1. You must have a variety of different relationship experiences with others to see how you care for them and how you care for yourself. You will experience hurt, pain, anger, betrayal, rejections, and/or shame within the most trying relationships because these are the places that require the most love within you, and within the other.

2. You must have interests, gifts, curiosities, and hobbies to learn more about yourself — and to love your unique abilities! The journey of life is to go deeper into your own essence and discover your buried treasures. Every person has multiple talents to offer and share. What is your passion? What brings you joy?

3. You must have a career or professional life in order to contribute to society, and as a result, you receive financial energy to pay for your lifestyle. Working is a wonderful gift. Being of service to others in any capacity gives your daily life a focus.

4. You must have a family who prepares you for greater healing and self-knowingness. Every person on the planet is here because of a merging between female and male sexual energies. Every person comes into existence already connected to a genetic

lineage. This family is chosen by your soul to assist your growth, healing, and evolution.

You must have all of these attributes, and more, in order to fulfill your soul purpose of elevating all areas of life to greater love. And to be realistic, some areas of life will be harder than others to transmute. There are some people you may struggle with loving for your whole lifetime. There may be some lessons and wounds that take a really, really long time to heal. There may be parts of yourself you can't come to terms with, or you constantly fight against, or you can't accurately see yourself. Some areas will require more time, effort, and devotion.

It is okay to do as much as you can with what you have. Be gentle and kind to yourself.

You do not have to do it all, even if you quietly expect that of yourself. At a soul level you are always doing the best you can. There is no 'hurry up and get this done' perspective from your soul because you are loved for simply being present and participating in the life experience.

Consider that for a moment: *You are deeply loved simply for participating.*

You showed up. You arrived in your human outfit because you raised your hand and said "Let me into THAT party." Then you checked your coat at the door, grabbed a glass of champagne, and strutted (or shimmied) into this celebration by choice. You chose to be a valuable contributor to the amplification of love and light on the planet.

So be kind to yourself as you move through the relationships, phases, and experiences that seem to pushback on you. Be gentle with your inner dialogue. Speak words of appreciation to yourself; words that are strong and confident. Know that you are always doing your very best and that is just perfect. Perfectly-perfect at all times, in all ways.

Take a moment and feel the energy of unconditional love. If nothing else, all you need to do is tap into that energy and breathe. You will instantly feel a high-vibe connection to your Self-love and Soul purpose energy.

Another part of your soul purpose – and you may not be expecting this one! – is to love form and matter and everything you perceive with your five senses. As you seek and question your spiritual side, remember also to bask in the joys of daily life. The physical world is a beautiful place and there is much to appreciate. Your soul can only have the sensations of your five senses because you are in a glorious body, so make time to love everything you touch, feel, hear, eat, and smell. Your Soul cherishes these connections. Are you taking time to love them, too?

Upon understanding that your soul purpose is to elevate everything to the vibration of love, you probably have another question (or three) to pose: But what about how I spend my time? How can I be of service? How do I know I am following my highest path? How can I share my gifts and contribute to the world in the best possible ways? What is my career path?

Everyone has these questions at some time on their path. But let me clarify something:

These are actually life purpose questions, not soul purpose questions.

Your life purpose is composed of your soul purpose, but your soul purpose is not based on your life purpose.

As a human being, you are embodying a personality. As a soul, you are unlimited energy. See the difference? Your life purpose is to include love in everything, but your soul purpose doesn't care HOW you do that. Just do it!

To find your life purpose, do one simple thing: Follow your passion. Or as Joseph Campbell said, "Follow your bliss."

The next thought you may have is, "But I don't know what my passion is."

Then you *get* to make finding your passion a priority. Start with what naturally calls to you. This is an integral component on the journey of knowing yourself, and it is not meant to frustrate you. If you feel frustrated, you are being too hard on yourself to find a specific answer. Your passion may *not* be a specific hobby, or a professional role, or an athletic activity. Your passion may be wide, and huge, and beyond any cubicle walls. Your passion may be a feeling. Or an inspiration. Your passion may be a creative focus, or volunteering your time on the weekends, or organizing garages. Your passion may be practicing a holistic lifestyle, or preparing vegan food, or grooming dogs at the animal shelter. Your passion may be communing with nature, or writing poetry, or fixing lawn mower engines. Your passion may be travelling the world, or watching birds, or tending to the school's annual activities, or selling home goods to groups of women in beige living rooms. Your passion could be anything, so enjoy the discovery process. Be open to new experiences that feel deliciously good. Follow where you feel a natural inner smile. Follow the effortless energy of being in that experience.

Once you identify your passion, you connect it to your life purpose by sharing it in some manner. Give it away, teach, volunteer, donate, host, gather, inspire, sell, connect. Turn your passion into service, and watch what changes in amazing ways. As you serve others through your passion, you step into your life purpose and share more love - naturally.

Your life purpose is to offer your energy out into the world as a gift through your passion.

Your soul purpose is to love yourself as you move through this experience called life.

Both of these understandings connect you on a deeper level to your personal truth. But as you voyage along through life and connect with other people, what happens when your personal truth does not match up with the truth of someone you love?

A big choice point is presented.

TRUTH AS A CHOICE POINT

IF ONLY FEELING STRONG IN our truth always felt powerful. I would love to profess that when we trust ourselves and believe in our own personal truth, life gets easier. But unfortunately, that is not always the case at times.

One powerful lesson I learned about truth was experienced through a life-changing heartbreak. I could write out the full diary version, but instead I will distill the story down to the heart of the matter: the other person's truth excluded choosing me.

For over a year, I had stayed in a dysfunctional workplace for heart reasons. It can be bizarre the things you do when you love someone and want to be with them every day, despite the turmoil and frustrations. Yet I remained hopeful.

Don't give up before the miracle. It could still happen.

The miracle breakthrough between us did occur with the relationship progressing forward. But then it quickly turned out to be a mirage. He said he had loved me for years, but stated, completely unexpectedly, that I was second best to a potential person in the future who would line up with his family's belief systems. The purity of our connection and the real love that existed between us was not enough. I was not truly an option as a life partner because his perceived choices – his truth – excluded me.

Rejection hit my heart hard for this shocking reversal, while judgment slammed into my head as a message that I was too different, outside of the boundaries of what was deemed "right" by his group of people. For all the ways I could intellectualize these messages, they both hurt deeply. I thought this person was the love of my life. I did not know what the next phase of my life looked like, but I did know that rejection and judgment were my current teachers.

When we are rejected, it is often based on more than meets the eye. We all make decisions based on what we believe our viable choices are, and the possibilities for those choices begin in our personal truth; our personal belief systems. Relationship decisions are one big area where these choices come alive in us, even in unconscious ways. What you believe is possible, or right, or best in relationships are built on your belief systems. Belief systems form your truth. Then choice points reveal our truths. Rejection reveals where belief systems and personal truths do not line up.

The most common response to rejection is the simple statement: "It is not personal". Yes, yes, I certainly get that. Different types of rejection affect us on different emotional levels. Some experiences of rejection are swift, objective, and cleaner to move through; they do not hit as hard in the heart or make a dent in our well-being. We glide through them and can easily adapt to "it is not personal" because we mentally understand what happened.

But that is not always how rejection *feels*. In this instance, the rejection felt completely personal. It hit my heart, deflated my hope, and then slowly sank my spirit. This is where the work lies.

How we *feel* about a personal rejection reveals where, on a deeper level, a part of us agrees with that message we are receiving. The rejection hits home because you are agreeing with their message in some way, too. You are interpreting rejection as a belief that you are not worthy, or not loved, or not valued as a person, or whatever external message you are perceiving. That deep feeling of rejection reveals where more healing is being required within you in order to rise above that perceived message and reconnect with something higher within you.

Here is an example. You get a new haircut that is a very different style, or new color, for you. The hairstylist finishes with the cut, whips you around to look at yourself in the mirror, and you love it. You feel good about your fresh look in a strong, empowering way, as if it is the new, real you. You can't stop smiling. It is the best hairstyle you have had since you tried "the Rachel" cut in the late 1990's.

Then you meet a friend for lunch and she gives you a questioning glance. "What did you do to your hair? I don't know if it's you. I think your long hair looked beautiful on you. I liked that better. Hopefully this will grow out soon."

You reply with confidence. "Oh I love this shorter cut! It's fresh and different, and I've been ready for a change. I am so happy with it!" Big smile still plastered across your face.

Your friend's opinion remains the same, but you do not agree with it because your truth is that you look fantastic. Her rejection of the style slides off your back and does not stick on you. You feel strong in your truth. (Of course, having to replicate that exact same look tomorrow without the stylist's talents is another matter.)

You have rejected her rejection. You have rejected that

energy.

Now take that same scenario where you have a new hairstyle, and imagine that you are not confident about this new cut. You like it, mostly, but you are not quite comfortable with the "new you". Maybe short hair is not right for you. You do not know what you believe about it yet.

You meet that same friend for lunch, and in the same scenario, she gives you her questioning glance and speaks the same words. "What did you do to your hair? I don't know if it's you. I think your long hair looked beautiful on you. I liked that better. Hopefully this will grow out soon."

Her rejection of this new style hits you hard because you are not strong in your own self-acceptance. Yes, yes, you know mentally that she is entitled to her own opinion. But you feel hurt, ugly, and take her thoughts personally.

You have accepted her rejection. You have accepted that energy.

The most important message is not from her, it is from within you. Your truth is in your feelings.

Changing your hairstyle is not as emotionally intense as matters of the heart, of course, but the feelings and energies of rejection can be the same. Your feelings show you where you need to meet more of yourself to claim what is true for you. Everything is energy. When an energy is weak within you, another person's energy can reflect or amplify that weakness.

Now take this same example and apply it to relationships. When you are your beautiful self, and someone rejects you, it is okay for it to hurt. The feeling is real, and it should not be denied. Honor what you feel. It is not something that can be mentally or intellectually resolved because it is in your heart. Your mind and ego have no dominion over the heart's terrain. Yet it is your ability to rise up into higher feelings of self-love that will dispel those hurtful ones. When the feeling of self-love is stronger within, you will embrace a stronger response with greater ease. Your inner message around that rejection will then come from a place of strength and confidence. You can develop responses that support how you feel and honor your truth, such as:

"Even if you do not believe that I am a good choice as a partner, and that I am second best to an imaginary person in the future, I know I am ready to be in a relationship with someone who is open and accepting of who I am right now. And you're an idiot." (Okay, maybe don't verbalize that second line.)

"It hurts to not be chosen by someone I love, but I reject the message of his rejection because it is not true for me. That truth is too limiting and small for how I want to live my life. And he's an idiot." (Oops, it came out again.)

"That message of being rejected and judged is not in alignment with my truth and choices. Someone else will meet me in a more open, loving space. Also, he's an idiot." (Sometimes these keyboards just have a mind of their own, I swear.)

You heal rejection more quickly when you acknowledge the pain and truth of your feelings, then follow it up with acknowledging your self-acceptance and self-love.

You heal when you develop an internal override system that does not agree with that external message.

You heal rejection by accepting yourself more.

You heal rejection when you stop agreeing with a conditional truth within yourself, even if it was unconscious and hidden.

You heal rejection when you no longer believe what is

untrue for you.

Your choice point is deciding to move through the pain, rather than sit in it, and to arrive at a higher place of self-love and self-acceptance in yourself.

This is the journey to unconditional love.

It can still hurt to be rejected and it takes time to heal from a deep pain, but you do not stay in that place. You move through it because your own truth is stronger. It is a guiding force that overrides the external message.

How we *feel* needs to be honored. Develop a higher truth within yourself to rise up and support you, love you, and guide you forward. Your own truth then becomes more connected to unconditional love.

So how do we heal judgment?

Judgment stems from conditioned programming that says there is a wrong and right for *everything*. Judgment does not consider other possibilities, other choices, all shades of gray, or other colors. Judgment rejects anything that could potentially threaten, weaken, or harm what is believed to be 'right'. Judgment declares boundaries on love. Judgment can create the feelings of shame, persecution, being ostracized, or being wronged. It comes from fear.

However, judgment only has power when we agree to participate in those boundaries and we do not push back with greater love. The healing comes from stepping outside that smaller judgment energy and opening up with greater compassion, acceptance, and love.

We heal judgment by expanding it into love.

The love we have within ourselves is the only amount of love we can extend out into the world. If you hold 75% judgment within you and only 25% love, you can only offer 25% love externally. You can only give what you have internally cultivated. But as you evolve judgment away from strict boundaries or small evaluations of right and wrong, then you can expand it beautifully into more unconditional love.

The grandest declaration we can offer another person is unconditional love. The true work is being able to say, "When you judge me, when you reject me, when you make other choices, when you send an unloving message, I can still love you unconditionally. Because that is how big my heart is and that is the energy I choose to walk with in this world."

When you claim unconditional love as your truth, it changes everything. It changes the energy within you, which then changes the energy you can extend out into the world. You begin to see other people with compassion because they are doing the best they can and they have the right to determine their truth. You relax into a deeper acceptance of everyone's journey being exactly what they want to create for themselves. You love them without conditions no matter conditions they put on you.

Rejection, judgment, and pain all take us away from our natural state of love. They can hurt so deeply because we know, at a deeper soul level, these feelings are not "us". They are not our normal energetic state of unconditional love. They are messages that have put conditions on our value, our worth, or our sense of self. Your most powerful choice points come when you decide what is true for you: conditional love or unconditional love?

Professor Rejection and Master Teacher Judgment showed me where I needed to get stronger in my own practice of unconditional love. I needed to cement in those potholes and strengthen up the weak areas. I have now come to believe that all relationships are guidepost and milestones on the path to unconditional love. It is our job to feel our honest emotions around painful experiences, and then move through the feelings so we can accelerate on to unconditional love: for ourselves, the other person, the growth, the experience, the healing. The highest versions of ourselves reside in the stillness and grace of unconditional love, but this human experience sure does a good job of taking us away from that sanctuary.

Relationships can be the ultimate playground with truth because there are many conditions that are applied to how it "should" look. When there is conditional acceptance there cannot be unconditional love. It actually took me a long time to get over that heartbreak because of how deeply it hurt and everything that was wrapped up in that situation. Moving forward based on my truth was the guiding torch; the flame kept burning stronger. I am grateful to now have a true partner who is independently strong, does not cave to family or peer pressure, and who is supportive of my work in the world, among many other wonderful qualities about him. There are no conditions on me to fit into a certain mold; there are no conditions on him to be a certain way in the world.

As time goes on, and you do not hold emotional intensity around a situation, it can evolve into something else. You can start to unconditionally love someone who put conditions on you. You can unconditionally accept who they are, or who you knew them to be, and allow that acceptance to be brighter than ever. You do not reflect conditions back to them, in other words. You find the best and leave behind the rest, not because you are trying to be the bigger person, or you have extra sprinkles on your sundae. It comes from your personal truth that declares, "This is who I am in the world" – and that is all you need to feel a bigger sense of love and acceptance. No recognition, no ego attachments, no external validation. It is how *you* choose to walk in the world. It is a reflection of *your* choice point.

With growing personal conviction, unconditional love becomes your guiding truth. You open up to accepting and loving what is and who that person is, even when their truth does not match your truth. You do not put conditions on them, nor yourself, and you then make solid choices from that place within you. I believe this is where the "it is not personal" feedback fits in properly because it is not personal to you when you can rest assured that you are loved no matter. You are connected to an even bigger force; a brighter torch of light.

If you do not feel strong in your truth at times, just be gentle with yourself. It will get more solid. When you work through what is taking you away from unconditional love, then you establish what is true for you regardless of anything outside of you. Most importantly, be mindful of how you carry these energies within yourself, or against yourself. *Are you rejecting who you are? Are you judging yourself?*

This painful heartbreak has benefited me in my work, too, as I now connect with really amazing, strong people who are way showers in their own lives. As a result of their leading roles, they have been on the receiving end at times of personal judgments, rejection, and painful shaming for who they are in the world. The pain can run very deep and be hard to move past when the wound feels so personal. Together, we embark on a very powerful process that heals and softens those places that need more love. I remind them that your only responsibility is to follow YOUR truth. That is your power; that is your self-respect to honor; that is your choice point. Even if you are experiencing judgment or rejections from others, please make sure you are not judging and rejecting yourself.

Instead, find where it feels more powerful to stand strong in what you see and feel as your inner truth, and then extend that love out to the other. *Move in that direction. Go towards that light.*

Healing rejection and judgment individually is one small way we contribute to healing both energies in the collective. I believe, without a doubt, that all spiritual truths are meant to lead humanity towards more love in our lives, and not to shut down any love and acceptance in the present. I also believe that every spiritual belief system is a winding path filled with love and lessons, hurt and healing, faith and fear, safety and struggle, open doors and closed windows, and a smattering of all kinds of people. I do not think we ever completely avoid those parts of life, no matter which path we take.

It is our conscious choice to hold ourselves accountable in practicing unconditional love and acceptance on whichever path we are on right now. When someone's choices exclude you, you see their truth. You also have a choice to make around what is true for you as you move forward. Acceptance rises. Rejection sinks. Unconditional love rises. Judgment sinks. What is your guiding truth? Rest assured, someone else will meet you in that higher, love-based energy to reflect your truth back to you.

Choice points based on your truth will shape your life. Expanding your truth to include more unconditional love after a painful time will help change the world. And if you need support getting to that place and trusting what messages you need to hear, sitting with your emotions is a great way to practice feeling your truth.

SITTING WITH YOUR EMOTIONS

HOW DOES JOY FEEL WITHIN you? What does confidence feel like in your body? How do you visualize success in your mind? All of these energies, and more, are natural elements within you, yet it may be perceived that they begin externally. Not so.

Take a moment right now to describe the sensation of joy – how does it feel rippling up your spine? Now hone in on the feeling of success – does it make your posture straighter and your smile wider? How does confidence affect your mood when you access it within your heart? Are you ready to take on the world with your light?

Each of these energies is a component of you and your light, and they require your attention. When was the last time you sat in the experience of your own joy, success, and confidence as they intermingled through your whole body? Take a moment right now to sit in this special cocktail of sensations and activate these parts of yourself. They will come alive as you focus on them. They will burst forth with a desire to be expressed!

Like the vibration of unconditional love, it is essential to connect with the energies you wish to experience. You must call on them and activate them intentionally. They wait for your initiation more than you know! How much time can you spend focusing on them? It may literally change everything in your life, including your unconscious emotional programming.

Transmuting all temporary emotions to higher expressions of love, forgiveness, compassion, peace, and joy is a lifetime theme for every person. These are all parts of your truth. Along the way, you will regularly need to work with parts of your emotional programming to fine tune it to these higher frequencies because we live in a dynamic world where energies are always in motion, similar to global weather changes. Nothing is constant.

Every person is composed of a variety of emotional imprints that dominate their life experiences. Think of the person who is always cheerful; the individual who always complains; the co-worker who is always stressed out. Emotional imprints are often habitual and unconscious, and typically accepted as "who that person is." Yet you, nor anyone else, is truly that emotional imprint. You are probably unconsciously activating that energy because you did not know you can reprogram yourself to take it to a new place. How do you move an emotional imprint to a new expression? How can you change something if you do not know what to change it to? You need a destination in mind, similar to getting in the car and driving somewhere new. You must connect with a higher emotional expression, such as joy, forgiveness and peace, so you have an idea of where the lower emotion is going.

Take a moment to call in your energetic expression of unconditional love again. Breathe in and breathe out as you embody this feeling. This connection to unconditional love is your destination point at any time for temporary lower emotional experiences. Creating a new destination point directs energy towards the vibration so it doesn't run amuck or get unconsciously thrown around. Many people unconsciously throw energy around at times because it is, well, unconscious. They are not mindful of what they are doing or aware of how their words, actions, or emotional expression is creating an impact.

Another way of saying this is that they are not aware of their own power. When you create a new destination point for emotional energy, you automatically connect with your innate power in the present moment.

Sit with the feeling of being powerful. What does that emotionally feel like for you? Perhaps you feel solid and sturdy; calm and balanced. Feel this power rising in your body, from your feet to your head, and then visually run the energy down to your legs, then into the earth.

Take a moment to sit in this state.

Now imagine the energy of your heart emitting a very high frequency of light as it forms a globe around your body. This globe of light exists all around your body and encapsulates your full energy field. Close your eyes to sit in this energy.

Now visualize your crown chakra a foot above your head, pulsing and alive with a violet color. You may see your crown chakra as a violet ball; now imagine the violet ball turning into a medley of flames. Visualize your crown chakra as a powerful violet flame. Sit with this image for a moment to absorb it in your mind's eye.

The violet flame transmutes energy. As you envision yourself holding your own personal violet flame energy, you can imagine sending your lower emotional expressions to this place. Like tossing trash into a bin, toss your temporary lower emotional expressions into the violet flame that you carry. Practice this when you are having a bad day, or you are feeling agitated with a person. Practice this before responding in a difficult situation, or as you take a deep breath during an intense moment. Give yourself a moment to breathe and visualize sending unconscious reactions up to a higher place.

This is a self-contained process that supports honoring yourself while also consciously choosing where your energy goes. With this exercise, you can transmute any emotions into a higher expression of love, compassion, forgiveness, peace, and joy. It is essential to have a strategic process for taking care of your emotional well-being.

Related to this is the underlying need for emotional self-reliance. Emotional self-reliance is a common life theme for those healing deep family wounds that originated in childhood. Perhaps you didn't receive the emotional care, nurturing, validation, and connection to your needs that a child requires and deserves. You may have unconsciously tried to compensate for this emotional lack by relying on others too much, or you may be continually seeking validation from others for your emotional experiences. It is up to you to self-evaluate your emotional programming and determine if you over-rely on external validation instead of internal affirmation. Emotional self-reliance may be an ongoing theme in relationships as you strengthen your ability to give yourself what you need.

Some people may have the opposite habit of only relying on yourself and not trusting anyone else with your emotions. As you grow in self-love and listening to your needs, you will attract trustworthy people into your inner sanctuary that you can open up to in safety. Sharing your heart with others in a safe way will relieve you of unconscious emotional energy you are carrying in your auric field. You will feel a lightness when you share. You will feel connected, supported, and heard in new ways. By evaluating your emotional patterns, you will determine what needs to be fine-tuned to ensure you are serving yourself in healthy ways. It takes great courage to change unconscious programming and step into a new way of being in the world.

Emotional wounds are often the most vulnerable spots in our lives. But at this time, please know in your heart, mind, and spirit that it is essential to work with emotional energy and transmute what you are carrying into unconditional love. All fears, doubts, self-judgments, criticisms, guilt, shame, and inner angst can be re-programmed into light when you commit to making changes in your emotional patterns. As you sit with yourself and observe your emotions, you will gain greater clarity around what no longer serves you. You can change yourself at any time.

It takes great courage to embark on this part of the journey because you are opening up to your vulnerable places—and this can be scary. Yet the only way out is through, and you deserve to be living in your full vibrant essence. Your light is guiding you through any emotional turmoil. Your light is alive with love for you as you do this work. You have everything you need.

So let's look at how to work with the most uncomfortable feelings. These may be the parts of yourself that you deny, or hide, or ignore, or avoid because on some level you don't want to deal with them. But even this is a fallacy because you do not have to "deal with them." All you need to do is listen to them.

Call in your vibration of unconditional love. Close your eyes and envision this energy surrounding you right now. Inhale and exhale the essence of love.

Now, as you sit in this high-vibrational state, choose a feeling that comes up regularly for you. Sadness? Pain? Anger? Criticism? Doubt? Insecurity? Trust whatever is calling to you. You are completely safe and protected to meet this feeling because you are surrounded by huge doses of unconditional love.

Ask the feeling to sit next to you on the couch. How does it look: Small? Hunched over? Tired? Dark? Huge and imposing? Describe how the feeling looks with the eyes of a neutral observer.

Then ask the feeling to speak to you.

What messages does it want you to hear?

Simply listen to the feeling. Hold it. Honor what it is telling you.

When the feeling is done speaking and grows silent, bring it into your heart and love this courageous part of yourself. Reply with self-love and acknowledgement:

"It is okay to feel (enter emotion) about this situation. I hear you. I validate your experience. I acknowledge your truth. It is perfectly acceptable to cry/rage/write/talk this through more."

Remember to breathe. Continue to honor what the feeling is saying if there is more. Listen to it. Validate it. Acknowledge that this feeling is real and alive within you. The messages you are receiving are gifts of deep wisdom. Allow it to be. Don't fight it; don't scold it; don't make it less than, or wrong, or not true.

Just love it.

Sitting with your emotions and loving them is vital to your whole essence. When you move through this listening process with love, you clear out the energy signature of that feeling. You have successfully heard its messages and have accepted this part of you. It is now a fulfilled part of you that has received validation. You then allow it to flow away, like a leaf on a river, or you send it up to your own personal violet flame to be transmuted into peace. The feeling no longer clouds your mind, or suffocates your energy, or weighs on your heart because it has been loved.

Sitting with deep emotions requires great courage and vulnerability. You must venture into new parts of yourself that were previously denied, unacknowledged, or pushed away. Beginning this practice may be a hard place to start. Many lower aspects of self may fight off the experience of sitting with your emotions because it is unknown, scary, and challenging to the ego-based identity.

As you practice active listening to each of these emotions, you will see how they are strands of yourself requiring more connection to unconditional love. Like individual kites flying recklessly in the wind, when you bring them into your love-filled essence, they calm down and feel safe. The emotions are heard. You provide a safe harbor for their expression and it frees the emotion from density. They finally feel loved.

Think of this as tending to your inner garden. You nurture and sow what is beautiful within you, while also picking out the weeds and removing the clutter that can creep in at times. Making time to nourish this inner garden will support the overall health of your world. Clearing emotional imprints that are not yours, or that you no longer wish to carry, will change your vibration. You will feel in command of yourself in new ways. Your perception of yourself will evolve. Your priorities will shift because what once grabbed your attention or weighed you down will no longer exist. A fresh sense of inner power will infuse your presence. You will lighten up. You will claim all aspects of your being with greater joy. You will experience more unconditional love as your guiding truth.

Now that you have cemented in this practice, it is equally important to return other emotions, energies, and lower truths back to their original sender when they are not connected to your ongoing practice of unconditional love.

RETURN TO SENDER

YOUR TRUTH HOLDS THE FREQUENCY of many gifts, including the importance of discernment, responsibility, and self-respect. Being a spiritual explorer opens you up to many new aspects of yourself that feel empowering, inspiring, uplifting, and love-filled. It is a joy to experience such high-vibrations within yourself. But as you open up to dormant areas within your energy field, you can also unconsciously open up to others who do not carry a high vibration.

Discernment is the ability to choose what is best for you. A wide variety of energies exist on the planet, and you have the ability to consciously choose what you wish to connect with. However, it is recommended that you have a blockage system that rejects energies you do not wish to receive.

Standing strong in yourself and loving yourself more requires strong boundaries. This is not a new understanding; in fact, many of you have built your lives around developing the boundaries skill. The intention with boundaries is to keep your self-love vibration as high and pure as possible by not allowing external energies to dilute it unnecessarily.

Realistically, there may be some days that are harder than others to do this, and that is okay. It is to be expected as the cosmic weather changes and dynamic events unfold. You may find yourself struggling with boundaries one week when you felt you had mastered them last week. Working with boundaries is an ongoing practice because there are many different types of energies in the world that do not fall into certain, or known, categories. You are always learning and growing, so you will always find yourself in a new experience of some sort. You will navigate each instance with perfection and you must be loving to yourself as you reinforce what you need. Your increased responsibility to your own energy and personal truth is a pillar of self-love.

The moment you are feeling unpleasant energies, or energies that you do not wish to intermingle with, from other people, simply call in floods of white light from above. Allow the light to shower you.

If you are alone, state aloud that this is not your energy and it must go back to its original source. Declare the energy to leave now.

Lower vibrational energies can slither and sneak about undetected, which is why you must trust what you *feel* even if it does not make sense. When something seems off, and you don't wish to connect with it, you can withdraw your energy instantly and cover yourself with light. Even while sitting in a boardroom, at a meeting, in traffic, at a conference, or attending a family reunion — you can always surround yourself with light.

It is more critical than ever to declare a loud energetic "No!" to anything you do not want to connect with. You can respond in your mind or with verbal words for any energy to *Return To Sender* with love, consciousness, and peace. Energy always honors your free will and responds in kind.

Consequently, when you send unwelcomed energy

back to its original source, you are gifting that person with the opportunity to know themselves better, if they wish. They may start to see a pattern in their life, or notice a reoccurring emotion, or begin to question why they keep having the same experience over and over again. Returning energy to sender is an act of respect for you and for the originator. How they respond or interpret the energy return is not your responsibility, nor is it your business. But it is to show you that establishing firm energetic boundaries with love-based intentions offers gifts to everyone if they are open and willing to receive greater conscious insights. Everyone potentially grows when you take care of yourself.

It would be wise to do a *Return To Sender* practice daily. Energies accumulate throughout the day, and just like taking a daily shower, you want to be mindful of your energy grooming habits. Before going to sleep, call in white light to surround you, like a cocoon, and require that all energy that is not your own be *Returned To Sender* with love, consciousness, and peace. Call in whatever uplifts you — angels, spirit guides, beings of light, master guides, the Holy Spirit — and ask for assistance in this clearing for the highest and best of all.

Nature demonstrates this function by pushing along the rainclouds and storms with powerful gusts of wind. The continual motion of jet streams around the globe keeps air flowing, as nothing is meant to remain stagnant or still. Imagine pushing unwelcomed energy up and away into the westerly winds, to fly with the natural forces of the planet, and to be transformed into rain that benefits the earth.

As *Return To Sender* becomes a more regular practice, you will feel a new lightness in your being and a softness in your essence. These are your connections to your own light growing stronger, even as you meet new faces of unconditional love.

THE OTHER FACES
OF UNCONDITIONAL LOVE

A S GREAT ENERGY SHIFTS CONTINUE to unfold around the globe, you must stand stronger in the presence of your own truth. You must hold unconditional love for yourself even when you do not experience it externally or receive it in the outer world. You are responsible for this Love energy within yourself, and yet there will be times when you come up to others who cannot see your vibrant heart or love-based intentions. They just cannot meet you in that space. And they won't.

The true gift in these instances is looking at how much value *you* place on another's viewpoint of you. Perhaps the bigger questions are: Why are you requiring others to see you a certain way? Why are you expecting them to be what they are not? Why are you asking them to agree with your self-definition?

It is the ego and unhealed inner child that requires others to see you in a certain way. These unconscious energies seek acceptance, approval, love, validation, and acknowledgement from outside sources because they are undeveloped aspects of yourself that have not been consciously connected to your unlimited well of self-love.

When the unhealed inner child receives conscious love from the mature adult part of you, the need for acceptance is then fulfilled and satisfied. With the Ego mind, the mature adult part of you must also step in to provide objective feedback about the unconscious loop of energy validation you are seeking outside yourself. You can consciously change these unconscious habits around by paying attention to where you seek acceptance and approval from others.

Others can only see you based on the vibrations they hold of themselves. If they feel inadequate, they will look to you as competition. If they are hurting, they may try to hurt you to distract from their inner pain. If they feel powerless, they may wish to "de-throne" you in some capacity to obtain a sense of power. Because of these energetic facts, you will wisely know who can see you and who cannot. You cannot give a blind man new eyes.

The experience of not being seen or valued can be temporarily hurtful, or infuriating, or damaging because you come from a well-intentioned place. You naturally seek peace and acceptance in relationships with others. You want others to live a joy-filled life, or to experience happiness, or to have the same passion for self-growth as you have.

Yet holding unconscious expectations of another is limiting for you and for them. You are essentially roping them into your needs. You are requiring them to give you something they are not capable of providing. This creates an attachment to them – either consciously or unconsciously – to be something they are not, which dishonors who they are in the present. Everyone is exactly where they need to be at all times. Every person is a soul with healing, lessons, and life choices. Is it not disrespectful to ask someone to acknowledge you if that is not part of their growth right now? Is it not presumptuous to expect another to hold a certain opinion of you? Is it not an infringement on their free will and soul choice? The need for others to be something they are not will lower your energy.

Instead, it is wise to simply acknowledge who someone is right now, at this moment in time, and accept them. Simply love them for being a fellow soul in a human body. Love them on a soul level if you do not love them on a human level. Honoring where each person is will free you from unnecessary emotional and energetic entanglements that do not serve you. Once this principle is understood, you may realize that connections to many people in your life are complete. You may see with fresh eyes that there are no shared interests with certain groups of people. But this is also divine and in perfect order. Unconditional love accepts without conditions.

As we come into our own truth in stronger and fuller ways, relationship changes typically occur in every area of life: friendships, romantic relationships, colleagues, associates, support groups. Many people may leave your personal orbit because your time together is complete. Sometimes you may choose to end the connection or perhaps they do. But like most types of breakup, it doesn't matter who selected it; it is still an experience of human detachment.

Human detachment is when we part ways with another person, be it a breakup, completion, passing, or just an energetic death. Human detachment can be a toughie. The laughter, support, joy, and connection that went into creating something precious is not an easy thing to let go of. Even when I have come to terms mentally and logically with why friendships are complete and relationships moved on, their little space inside my heart still lived on.

At their core, relationship changes are about energy changes. It is very simple, actually: Where you once connected to someone, the energy of your connection has changed and you are each at different places now. Not "good" or "bad" or "better" places – that is human judgment kicking in – but different places like spokes on a bike wheel. You can think of it as, "I moved out this way, while she moved out that way." "I went over here, while he stayed right there." "I made this choice about my personal growth, while they said another direction was best for them."

It is all energy in motion – swirling, moving, flowing – and we can "get it" on that level. But dang it, it is still hard to deal with at times because relationships encompass multiple layers and intersections. I have learned some mighty helpful ways to move through, and with, the energy ride of human detachment.

1. Find the Blesson of the relationship.
   What is a blesson, you say? The blessing and the lesson combined. Complete the sentences:
   "This relationship came into my life to help me...."
   "This relationship taught me to...."
   "At its core, this relationship was about..."
   Then say "Thank You, Thank You, Thank You" to that person's soul a million and five times. Or half that if you have to pick the kids up from school, or your coffee is done brewing, or the commercial break is over. When you identify what you healed, learned, or how you grew, you have just identified the blesson.

2. Remember that human detachment is the opportunity to strengthen unconditional love. Consciously move towards the love. Consciously remember that what you shared with someone can't be judged as anything less than perfect for you at that time in your life. It was perfect. Everything seen through the lens of unconditional love always is.

3. Send unconditional love to your wound. Or the loss. Or the hurt. Or the fear. It does not matter where the love is sent; it just matters that you are consciously creating and sending it. It is okay if you cannot do it every day or even regularly. In fact, it is very honest to recognize how you feel when the heart connection is struggling. But unconditional love is always waiting for you when you are ready to return to it.

4. Repeat this process daily, weekly, or whenever the sadness, longing, or missing them feelings come up. They can be triggered randomly and might never go away completely. But the process of moving towards unconditional love will speed up and be faster as it is repeated.

I have become better at moving through the feelings of human detachment by remembering these steps. It is a process, and some days it is still hard. I find myself sad, angry or stirring through old scenarios and mucky-muck.

So what do I do? I go for a bike ride.

I allow the two wheels with their ever-spinning spokes to support me. I allow the energy of change to move through my body and be released. I allow my heart the opportunity to say "thank you" a million and five times with each rotation and to remember the blessons. I allow everything to move. I allow everything to be unconditional love. I allow myself water breaks and slow leg stretches along the way. Then I get going again on my path with new strength.

By the time the ride is over, and I am sweaty and sticky and feeling "not-cute," I have returned to a higher understanding and appreciation. My path has featured many lovely souls who have joined me at important phases along this journey.

I am so grateful for everyone I have known and all of those whom I have allowed to know me. I honor their new place on the bike wheel spoke. I honor my new place on the bike wheel spoke. We are all exactly where we need to be.

We do not attract people into our lives to find their faults, or stay hurt, or be disappointed, or hold onto the past. We attract people to experience more love, joy and gratitude in the present.

For many of us, it is essential to be on parts of this journey alone at times. It must be this way at certain stages. How will you know yourself if not in solitude? How will you hear yourself if not in silence? How can you grow stronger if not by uncovering a weakness? How will you love your beautiful light if you are too focused on external energies?

Essentially, you are becoming wiser to the different types of consciousness on the planet. Not everyone is actively developing self-love at this time. Not everyone is growing, evolving, or even interested in their spiritual gifts. This is perfectly planned. Can you accept where they are at on this stage of their journey?

Let's play out a scenario where you attempt to engage with someone who does not see you. Perhaps you are committed to proving a point, or teaching them a lesson, or demonstrating your value, while they are committed to pushing back and resisting your energy because it is uncomfortable for them; they do not want to be forced to do or know or learn anything.

Imagine a boxing ring. If you step into a boxing ring with another, and both of you have your "dukes up" to make a point energetically, it opens both of you up to potential outcomes that may be mutually unsatisfying. You each have an agenda, and you each have the desire to be right on some level. The unhealthy ego is behind this need to prove, compete, win, and "have the last word" in the boxing ring. Both of you are operating in a lower energy field that will never satisfy you, even if it is seductively appealing to possibly "win" or demonstrate your worth.

Now imagine this same boxing ring and see yourself stepping into it with your hands in a prayer pose in front of your chest. See yourself energetically saying "Namaste" to the other person in the ring. They will have their fists raised as if to fight you, to prove you wrong, to prove themselves as stronger and right. Except you are not engaging in this dynamic. Instead, you are activating peace within yourself. You are visualizing light all around the boxing ring. You arrived in the space with the intention of honoring yourself and honoring them without needing to do anything. You have just brought greater peace to the situation with this simple intention.

Your logical mind may say that if someone steps into the ring to fight you, and you don't fight back, you will be knocked down. They will push over you – with their will, their opinion, their force—and do you harm. They will win. But you can change this limiting perspective around to see yourself as standing strong in your own energy, in who you are, and not needing to do anything because there is nothing to win in the first place. Winning is a message from your overactive ego; you are focusing on the message from your heart. You are choosing to create greater acceptance.

As you stand in the ring, imagine your peace-filled energy field being 30-feet tall instead of five feet tall. See it extend beyond the boxing ring and light up the whole arena. The energetic "fighter" across from you would then be surrounded by peace even when they are engaging in a struggle. You are showing up with acceptance for difference and honoring of *what is.* You are training yourself to not feel the desire to prove anything, It takes great strength to be powerfully peaceful in this situation. Some of the world's greatest leaders, such as Gandhi and Martin Luther King, Jr., took this approach to disagreements. They would hug their opponent and demonstrate love instead of engage in a conflict. Now you can energetically follow suit when you discern it is the best way to honor yourself and everyone.

You do not need to fight for peace. You peace for peace.

Be aware of when you are fighting for approval. Is it worth your energy?

Notice when you are directing too much energy towards a group for acknowledgment. Are you relying on them too much?

Observe when you find yourself quietly judging, criticizing, or scolding another. Is that the energy you want to consciously put out into the world?

Return back to yourself with acceptance for all. Find a bit more unconditional love and detachment within yourself. This will be easier said than done some days. There may be people who trigger you the rest of your life.

There may be permanent completions to long-standing relationships based on this wisdom. There may be days or weeks when you are firmly set on making a point and must demonstrate your point. But look at the gifts you are receiving in the process. These people and situations are making you so much stronger, wiser, and intentional. They are a gift.

Everyone is exactly where they need to be in their lives. Each person has free will and the ability to make the best choices for them—just like you do. The sooner you arrive at acceptance of who someone is in reality, in this present moment, the sooner you will experience peace for anyone who cannot see the real you.

And you will even feel a release energy because you understand that you don't require them to see you. You no longer hold that expectation or attachment to them. You don't need them to see anything at all. Instead, you choose to love your own presence even more. You consciously choose to connect with peace and acceptance within.

As you hold the wisdom that all is in perfect order and everyone is learning what they need to know, you will require less of others and their opinions. You will feel fortified on your self-love mission and return to your passion. Your heart will expand and your connection to the love vibration will strengthen. And then an amazing thing will occur! You will find a place in your heart that brings them in.

You will open up to greater unconditional love that includes everyone, no matter where they are on their path. You will open up your heart to accepting this present moment as it is. You will open up to loving yourself more for the ability to hold this space and the ability to be love-filled regardless of anything in the external world.

You will connect to your heart's energy of unconditional love and personal acceptance—and you will find that is enough.

OPENING UP TO
GREATER COLLECTIVE ENERGY

I LOVE ZUMBA, THE LATIN-inspired dance program that has become a worldwide fitness phenomenon.

At the three minute mark of every class, I am alive with how much I enjoy the workout: the rhythm, the moves, the music, the collective energy. The room is filled with non-stop music pounding against the walls and ceiling as over fifty bodies of all ages and sizes move in synchronized movement.

At the 12-minute mark, the music is louder and faster. My focus is greater. Breathing becomes more intense.

By the 33-minute mark, my heart is thumping wildly, more sweat beads are forming and my quads are sore from all of the deep squats. I feel a little tiredness beginning, but I have no desire at all to stop moving. There is something greater happening in these walls that pulls me through any temporary aches.

When I'm starting to feel the workout burn, I know it's time to consciously shift my attention to the collective energy in the room. I allow the energy of every pumping heart to lift me up and carry me through the intensity. I connect with energy bigger than my own body.

As I shake, turn, and step at the 41-minute marker, I remind myself that at every moment of the day, energy of every kind is circling the globe: High energy, low energy, stop-and-go, win-and-exceed, accomplish-and-finish energy.

A divine balance is always in motion. When I am feeling a little tired, others in the room are feeling invigorated. When I am feeling weak, others are feeling strong. When I am feeling uncertain, others are feeling absolute conviction.

There is always a way through our weak spots by connecting personal energy with the continual swirling movement of collective success and accomplishment. Not only is energy always circling the globe, but we can call on the energy of many to support us at any time with any goal. With this knowingness, there is a strategic secret available for success at any time:

Anything we want to accomplish is being successfully done right now somewhere in the world.

When we consciously shift our "right in front of me" perspective and tap into the dynamic flow of continual source, our abilities take on a whole new level of potential. Anything we seek to accomplish, grand or small, is possible. It is all connected.

I use these Zumba classes to not only invigorate my body, but to invigorate the energy of a bigger dream. I believe with renewed strength that I can write a book. In fact, it is happening now. And I have energetically connected myself to the bigger understanding that anything is possible in my life when I connect to the Universal forces that support any dream we want to experience.

1. Intention is everything. Clearly define and know your goal. Be specific about the end result.

During my hour of Zumba, working out is my intention, but I carry the energy forward into my other creative goals. I see myself as a writer among millions of writers. I am not alone in this goal, and that is inspiring. Staying focused on the end result directs the energy forward. Don't be distracted by *temporary* anything. Remember the main intention.

2. Visualize the energy of your goal circling the globe.

What you want to accomplish can be viewed as benefiting and serving people around the world. The energy of your goal is alive and moving *right now*. To make the energy easier to "see," visualize it as something beautiful and inspiring to you. Make it a color. Give it texture. See it as organic, alive, and in movement already, even if it is not in its final form yet.

3. Move with the force of that energy and see yourself as part of it.

Now see yourself as part of that energy you just visualized. Consciously put yourself in the movement and flow of that greater global force. Be it and feel it. During Zumba, I visualize a book benefiting the greater good as if it were already happening *right now*.

4. Release expectations of *how* and simply *do*.

How many chapters are left to write? How many weeks or months will it take me? How will I launch it out into the world? The mind wants to know exactly *how* an accomplishment will come about, but being connected to collective energy allows us to rise above the current minute and enjoy the full experience of a creative expression.

As long as I keep moving and going with the energy, all of the *how* questions will flow away. I just need to keep moving through each song (eyes off the clock!) and stay in the collective energy of the end goal. Simply do it and keep moving.

5. Remember what your energy is doing for others. They need you, too.

I hope that what I am learning through this creative process will help more people create what is in their heart, too. Even though I may feel tired at times, or start to worry, I remind myself that I can be strong and forge ahead in order to teach and share with more people. They may need my energy in order to push through an intense phase or to figure out a roadblock, too.

As we progress forward with a dream, there are people who can benefit from your strength and determination, too. Remember that you are a source of inspiration for others. Your desire to stick with your end goal benefits others even if you can't see it.

There is never a lack of accomplishment in the world. There is never a lack of potential. There is never a lack of success. But there can be a lack of *connection* to each of these qualities at times.

And that is precisely when it is time to connect to

other people's goal-oriented energy to carry you through. It is available whenever you choose it, simply by finding support groups, watching YouTube videos, studying, researching, and joining up with others who are seeking a similar result. The support for any dream is waiting for you right now with open arms and an expanding space. There is always room to accomplish anything and be more successful because it has the power to benefit more people in the long-run.

By the end of every Zumba class, my body, mind and spirit are always soaring. I make a mental note to take this morning accomplishment into my creative projects throughout the day. I am invigorated with the knowingness that many people will be successfully working away on creative projects at the same time as I am. I see that inspiring creative energy as so massive, sparkly and vibrant that it electrifies me with glee – and I'm so proud to be a contributing part of it.

My first book is coming together. There are a lot of questions and unknowns, but I am committed to it on a whole new level. I am closer than I have ever been and the growing momentum is exciting.

All of us in the Zumba class then file out of the building together, smiling, holding open doors, and offering well-wishes to each other. We exude a common glow and well-earned exhaustion after another successful session. It feels good to start the day with a worthwhile accomplishment and inspiration to keep writing.

Of course, there is one drawback to experiencing collective energy at the same time as everyone else. It is called a traffic jam in the Zumba parking lot.

EXPANDING YOUR ENERGY OUT
INTO THE WORLD

SINCE THIS TIME REQUIRES YOUR active, conscious participation in your truth, you will find yourself in situations where you will need to leave your mark, so to speak. You will need to speak up and say what is wrong, or what can be improved, or what is not in integrity. You will need to take a conversation to a higher level by leading it away from blame, anger, gossip, and other low-vibrational energies. You will know when you need to say something because you will feel it energetically, like a sudden spark of knowingness.

Guide others to higher ways of being themselves by showing them a higher side of you. Share your spiritual understandings or an inspiring perspective in practical, relatable terms. It may sound completely foreign to them and you may feel their discomfort. Do not force a conversation or an idea, but do not hold back, either. That is the main objective — do not hold back your light, your voice, your truth. It takes courage to expand your energy out into the world. Now it is time because thousands are doing it at the same time as you.

Your job is not to sell your truth, nor to tell someone what to believe, nor be righteous in your point of view. Rather, your job is to simply push yourself out there a little further and expand the energy of your consciousness. This is an energetic practice, and eventually it will be second nature. When your intention is love, anything you do from that pure place carries the vibration of love in unmeasurable forms.

Make a commitment to expand your energy even if it is uncomfortable at times. Not "uncomfortable" in the sense that you feel unsafe, but uncomfortable because you are stretching out of a comfort zone. You are learning new ways to use your energy and share it with love. You are pioneering into new frontiers and practicing a new version of self-love in the world. Your soul is celebrating this ability every day.

As you expand your energy out into the world, you will feel stronger in who you are. You will notice that less things affect you in the ways they did before. It is a combination of strength and softness that allows you to experience this new way of being in your own presence. You feel confident in saying your truth, sharing your ideas, or trying something new because you are guided by the energy of your light and self-love. You are living from this place and you want to share it with the world.

You will notice others expanding their energy as well, and it will make you happy. You will feel a soul connection and synergy with these like-minded souls because you are collectively changing the vibration of the planet. Embrace others who are sharing their light. Embrace the happiness and abundance of your friends and peer groups. Support the success of another's business, or relationships, or financial developments. Support all of the energies you wish to receive as well. You will continue to open up to these vibrations more effortlessly and witness magical developments unfold as your energy expands out into new territory.

Whatever you create within yourself, you create more of in the world. It is all interconnected and intertwined, a continual dialogue of energy of You and Us. When you look at how you can be more courageous, loving, peaceful, and happy within yourself, you've just created that same energy for everyone else to tap into, too. It is never only about you; that is not even possible. It always branches out to Us.

It absolutely matters more than you know. People are looking for the good vibes from well-intentioned energies. Or else why would any of us pay so much attention to Facebook?

It is never about you. It is always about you. This is the contradiction of our times as we move from our human selves to our spiritual selves and then back again. The flow is constant because we are healing separation between the two energies; uniting and integrating them within, and then applying that unification in all areas of life. We are journeying forward with unconditional love.

WHEN BELIEVING IN YOUR TRUTH
CARRIES YOU HIGHER

WHEN MY WEBSITE, ConsciousCoolChic.com debuted in 2011, I was both ecstatic and anxious because there were no other websites on consciousness out there. That may be hard to imagine now as there are many excellent websites featuring consciousness topics. A lot of blogs back then were focused on self-help, lifestyle, food, inspiration, crafts, astrology, and more, yet I had not found a spiritual website on consciousness, so who knew what would come of this idea. No guarantees, but hey, give it a shot. My spiritual journey began back in the early 1990's and I had nearly twenty years of spiritual study and information to start sharing– if I was ready? I felt a surging YES within my body, and that is when I knew I was ready for it. *Nothing to lose, Molly, just do it.*

I wrote about early metaphysical teachers, such as Florence Scovel Shinn, Emmett Fox, and Catherine Ponder; included book recommendations; and offered original affirmations. My blog posts focused on energy, astrology, and how the Universe is supporting you, and then I debuted content on the 12 Universal Spiritual Laws. Within months, people found the website, signed up for emails, joined the membership area (now closed), enrolled in classes, and asked for personal sessions. All great feedback. Good to see that the content was useful and connecting with people.

Yet as my website grew in homepage views and blog sharing, I started to be targeted by someone with a bigger following who duplicated what I offered. It could only loosely be called "plagiarism" (in legal terms) yet it was all too close for comfort to me. It smelled wrong. I had never followed her, or even knew what she was doing; I never read her books or even visited her website. I was not interested in her work because I had been there-done that years ago. In other words, she was never on my radar, but somehow I ended up on hers. I found out about it through other people. I paid it very little attention at the time and stayed focused on what I could create, offer, and share in the world, including publishing my first book.

Then a trend started to emerge. When I would discuss a topic or mention a spiritual teaching, within weeks she would be credited with very-very similar words in a social media post that was shared and popped up on my newsfeed. She has a much bigger following than I so her words went further than mine. I could find an objective perspective for all of this, as other people are certainly allowed to talk about anything they want and it could be similar to what I shared. None of us owns a topic. Fair enough. No big deal. Yet after unintentionally witnessing this happen five times, I did not think it was just a coincidence. Still a bit smelly.

When the Conscious Wisdom Festival (an online summit I created, produced, and hosted with numerous spiritual experts) was gaining momentum, she was part of a similar online summit with her Popular Metaphysical Kids who planned their last-minute event one week prior to mine. They used my event's emails and testimonials as their own.

When I was approached to support a person, project, or company and I agreed, she would show up as partnering with them weeks or months later. After four times of this happening, it was not simply a coincidence that out of all the people, companies, and places in the world, she would then be exactly where I was featured.

When my first book, *The Art of Trapeze: One Woman's Journey of Soaring, Surrendering, and Awakening* finally launched after years of struggling with writing, it actually took me three different attempts to figure out how to get a book out there into more hands. It was much harder than I thought to launch a first book. So I read, researched, studied, and asked questions about how other authors did it. After months of studying book marketing approaches, I finally figured out something that could possibly work. It blew me away to see over 28,000 book downloads come through in a few days. With absolute shock and gratitude, I posted about it on my blog and social media.

Then the one star reviews started coming in that were direct personal attacks at me and had nothing to do with the memoir. I received rude Facebook comments and mean email messages. Some of my most popular Facebook posts with thousands of Likes and one with 26,000 shares were reported to Facebook as spam. Facebook does not want to lose popular content. When I inquired with Facebook about these disappearances, they said it was reported by *x* number of people – the same number in her girl group.

I could be objective enough to see that when you become more successful, other people who want that same thing you obtained get competitive, or jealous, or they want to take you down because they feel threatened in some way. This happens in all industries, and the metaphysical world is no exception. Every person on the planet has an ego (except Elmo, perhaps). It all comes with the territory of working in the public sphere. It happens to many people, and it can be far, far worse. Receiving 1-star reviews is part of being an author. Not everyone is cheering you on. The haters show up when you start to get a lot of love. I could handle it all much better with this objective knowingness. I gave it time and just took deep breaths to step back. *This too shall pass, Molly. Don't be too attached. Keep working. Keep going.*

Privately, I cried. A lot.

On a human level – on a heart level – it fuckin' sucked. Every step forward felt like two steps back, professionally. To be *obsessively* targeted in such a way really rocked me. I did not even know her, never connected to her personally, and yet I was on the receiving end of such terrible stuff that I felt powerless around. I experienced these rolling feelings of powerlessness, anger, pain, and hurt. I was continually sabotaged and felt like a victim because I had done nothing to her: I never followed her, never read her books, and had never held any animosity to her. I knew she existed in this industry and that she was helping many people. She is mass market; I am more niche. Individually, we offer people more information to help them on their journeys. She does her thing over there... I do my thing over here. To each their own. My perspective is that there is room for everyone—but you cannot assume that is a truth everyone operates with in their life. Some people simply look to seek and destroy at the slightest whiff of being dethroned from their high perch.

A friend texted me that this person was on Dr. Oz talking about the same topics I had just covered in recent weeks. "Molly, didn't you *just* talk about that on your radio show last week? I swear she is saying exactly what you said." Perhaps that is so, and yet once again it was way too close for comfort. Television shows can be taped in advance; maybe it was another coincidence. Yet there was a definite pattern of this ongoing behavior from that one person.

Plagiarism is not simply in written form. It can be spoken words, teachings, guided meditations, radio show topics, and the general sharing of information that did not originate with that person, yet it is repurposed as one's own. An ongoing pattern of this behavior makes it even clearer. However, chances are high that if you are interested in what I share and teach, you would not come across the duplicate work because my audience and her audience tend to not overlap. She works with "newbies", and I support and guide people who have already been on their spiritual path for a bit. It is the difference between elementary school and college, and why would you visit a school that does nothing for you?

There were times when it all felt futile. What was the point of doing all of this work and creating my own content when it appeared to regularly be whisked away by someone else with a bigger following? Writing a book is a lot of work; maintaining a website with new offerings can be challenging; creating online courses takes more time than you expect; and everything online these days can easily be re-purposed by people with nasty intentions. The best outcome you hope for is that it reaches people who can benefit from it, and know that they can come back to you for more information and answers.

I kept hearing "ponzi scheme" with this energy dynamic, too. Such as, a Plagiarism Ponzi Scheme where someone intentionally takes, takes, takes and believes they have a right to do so because they have the power, connections, influence, and ego to keep it up. The energy around this game increases to the point where they believe they actually own the content because they are "in control" of it and can manipulate others into believing it, too. Yet when that fateful knock comes on the door from the Universe, they cannot support what they have created because it is all an illusion, a sham. And it is their followers who pay the price through loss of trust and doubting what they learned in the first place.

So on it went. The worst part was when she attacked me personally behind-the-scenes and in private circles, making crazy claims that I was the one who had copied or plagiarized her (or something along those lines). I went ballistic. *Do I laugh hard because it is all so ridiculous, or do I cry from exhaustion at this manipulation where the bully plays the victim?* My response was very simple: Go ahead and check my Kindle, check my bookshelves, check my IP address, check my browsing history, check my computer, check my tablet, check my brain—you'll find absolutely nothing related to her work, website, books, anything because her "teachings" offer me nothing of value.

A few really great people I had on my radio show as guests would not follow up, and then it became clear why… they had a connection to her. Due to her influence and high-level network, she was able to shut down potential opportunities for me with THE biggest people in the spiritual industry. Think of the most influential spiritual people who connect with millions, and then see those opportunities taken away. I heard it happen. I cried. My heart sank even lower. People who had no clue who I even was heard untrue negative things about me from her with the intention of damaging my professional reputation. She was ruthless.

And so the bullshit continued. I'll spare you the other examples. But clearly there was an ongoing pattern of abuse, obsessive targeting, and intentional harm directed at me that she perpetuated for years.

The message I felt was... *It is not safe to be myself in this industry.*

Because by being myself, I am attacked, stalked, and targeted. She has the power, influence, connections, and status in this spiritual business world; I do not.

Some days, I really admired ostriches. Just look at their ability to ignore the world and dwell in the comfort of their own little holes. Ignorance IS bliss at times, so I accessed my Inner Ostrich to carry on. Then I would knock myself straight and remember I am not a coward and I am no victim. *Inner lion, Molly!* Inner tiger. Inner bear. Inner unicorn! *Keep going.*

Now, I understand that it is normal to tell me to 'fight back' and 'take legal action' and 'stand up for yourself'. I agree – and I did the best I could with each of those tactics. If only it were that simple, and it was not, unfortunately. There are certain elements that need to be proven legally, and that can be tricky because it can be hard to prove what is needed, or even get people to speak on the record. Taking legal action would have involved spending a lot of money on lawyers with most likely very little to show for it. It was like walking in quicksand and continually sinking down deeper with every step forward.

This was also how I knew it was a spiritual lesson because the "typical" ways of fighting were not effective or applicable. All I could do was surrender and keep detaching, which sometimes brings you down to your knees before you rise up again.

So I clung to a driving belief:

The truth rises.

The truth always rises.

It may not happen quickly, or clearly. It could take years. It could be happening slowly in ways you never know. It does not even have to be something you see; it could just be a feeling that the truth is living out there and it eventually rises up into the light because that is what truth is made to do. It lives and breathes with purer air.

During those six years of being targeted and sabotaged behind-the-scenes, I kept my head down and worked. I focused on what I could control and what I could do with my energy. There are situations in life that are hurtful and we have no control over them…yes, we all know that is part of life. *So what can I do today?* I always had control over my ability to write, teach, share, podcast, create, and essentially carry on with my driving purpose. I put my energy into relationships with clients, peers, and really, really great people. I only talked about this situation with two people I trusted. I would not let it consume any more conversations than that, nor allow it to be a gossip thing.

Her competitiveness was trying to take me down and off of my path. Chances are high she has been competitive like this with other people, too. She could have really stopped me on this path if I did not already have a strong spiritual foundation that reminded me that I was here to be of service to many, and that decision was mine to continually choose – competitive bitches be damned.

Just carry on, Molly.

When the odds are stacked against you and it can easily feel like your efforts are pointless, you still have a choice point. So I decided to play it smarter. I held back publishing some of my books. I only posted 40% of my work publicly and withheld a majority of it for my clients only. I took screenshots of my Facebook posts in case they went missing. I downloaded all of my radio shows and podcasts so they could not be reported or removed. I reported and banned harassing lame people on Facebook. I denied sessions with people who were trying to get on my calendar with bad intentions. I kicked people out of a few classes who were snooping around maliciously. I shut down my communications to mutual people who were connected with her, trusting that if we needed to reconnect when all of this cleared out, then it would happen on its own.

One time, I made myself devilishly smile by publishing a hidden article on my website on a spiritual topic that was filled with false info. My readers would not find. It was just waiting for her or her assistant to grab it and take it back to their sisterhood. I do not feel any guilt around that.

I had sessions with trusted healers to clear what was mine while not naming names. I quite regularly asked, "What the fuck is her deal?" Talk about being given a huge opportunity to practice the Law of Detachment.

I prayed. *Show me. Show me what I need to know and learn from this.*

I was willing to claim whatever was mine in this dynamic, whether that was from other lifetimes when I was a bitch or a crazy lunatic or whatever role I played. I was willing to own it, even if I did not understand it, just to be sure I was covering all the bases and knocking on every door to find the answers I needed.

I practiced Ho'oponopono.

I continually let go of any expectations I was holding, consciously or unconsciously.

I asked for guidance and clarity about the best next steps.

I prayed to heal my own wounds around this

situation.

I took lots of long walks and deep breaths and exercised.

I felt gratitude for everything I had created and accomplished on my own, knowing how hard it has been at times.

I made sure to get out of my own head and keep focusing on how I could help other people, like my awesome clients and trusted friends. Your own mind can be a really terrible place to hang out at times. Hello, inner ostrich.

I checked my own ego at the door: *Molly, you don't have to prove anything. You don't have to fight for anything. You don't have to engage. Just be. Just keep going.*

And I strengthened my connection to God/Spirit/Source because I know that is my true connection to what is best for me going forward. No one else can duplicate, attack, or sabotage that connection except myself. Her deep powers of darkness would not diminish my high powers of light.

I declared that it WAS safe to be myself in this industry and not let her external power overtake my internal power. I would not let one person's ultra-competitive, obsessive behavior stop me from what I am here to do. Hell NO.

I kept clearing out the anger, pain, or hurt that came up in me. I made peace with the fact that if really popular "spiritual" people were like this, and not even walking their talk, then I am deeply grateful I did not work with them, or appear on their programs or shows or events. Everything is energy, so clearly there would not be a fit. I was proud to be different. I was damn proud to not be a Popular Metaphysical Kid because that shit is not cool at my lunch table.

So why am I sharing this story now?

Because just recently, this woman's energy was finally gone from my world. The person who had been staring at me with binoculars and a rifle had left the building (yeah, that's the image I got, bleh). After six years of stalking, sabotaging, and targeting me, she was truly out of my energy field.

Gone.

I felt it so clearly one morning; it was AMAZING. Oh, how I wish I could describe it for you... My whole being was light and free; like I could stretch my arms out and move and LIVE and there was nothing staring back at me. I called a good friend and she knew exactly what I meant. It had finally ended. I wish I could put the sensation of freedom into better words for you.

Gone.

Through my years of writing, publishing and sharing, I never held any expectations of fitting in with the Popular Metaphysical Kids and sitting at their lunch table. That is not really who I am. I like the freedom to do my own thing. I work fast and I do not want to be held back when inspiration strikes. Yet a small part of me acknowledges that some really awesome opportunities were shut down to me because of her slander and attacks on my professional reputation.

Maybe a few other things could have unfolded that would have reached and helped more people. There were things I dreamed about, like we all dream big, and those dreams just were not meant to be. There is disappointment that this individual took life-changing opportunities away.

But hey—maybe those opportunities were not a good fit for me in the long run, anyways.

I will never know, and it does not matter now. That

was not my path. This lesson was my path. I simply intended to write books on topics that I hoped could help people, and offer useful spiritual guidance to whomever was attracted to it. I am proud of what I have created and shared over the years. It has been filled with many highlights that I am grateful for, and huge blessings have certainly showed up, too.

Perhaps something else is underway that can be of better benefit? I still remain hopeful.

If she was truly a spiritual expert, then she would know how energy really works, which is that what you put out there comes back to you three-fold. Some teachings say nine-fold and ten-fold. Even when an intention starts off as a smaller thing, the more energy you feed it grows it exponentially. Those choices of playing with people's energy in any form have ramifications in our world that eventually boomerang back around with consequences. Just ask Bernie Madoff how it paid off to take people's money (energy) and say it was something more than it was.

When people make these choices, I have come to realize that they are working something out with God in their own world. They are in conversation with God around something, and they are fighting it, or denying it, or simply projecting it onto others so they do not have to work through it. This understanding can help you step back and remember what YOUR truth is in a situation.

The more important question to ask yourself is: What are YOU in conversation with God around? *You will know.*

Gratefully, I have learned and healed a lot.

With this experience, I was given the opportunity to practice neutrality and detachment even more. I do not feel like a victim or powerless anymore. I know what is mine—not from an egoic sense, but from an energy sense—cannot be taken, or duplicated, or stolen. And I can always go get more of my own energy and inspirations at any time, 24/7, as that supply is unlimited for all of us.

A common myth in spiritual circles that I believe is overused is the whole "you attracted this" phenomenon, as if a victim does something to attract a bully, or you are asking for a situation because of something you put out there. I have another explanation to offer.

When you are the Real Deal – in any field, in any profession, in any undertaking – you automatically threaten those who are not the Real Deal. They can be jealous, competitive, devious, and very determined to take back control because on some level of their psyche they feel the gig is up – the bar has been raised and they do not measure up. This is never totally true because anyone can grow and continue to be a better version of themselves. Yet their self-worth feels incredibly empty. From the outside looking in, this is also an invitation to see them and their God conversation with compassionate eyes. What a crappy feeling to experience, but this in no way justifies taking obsessive actions that cause harm. Maybe you have seen this in your own life as you step into the truth of who you are and improving yourself. You change the vibration of yourself and that sets some people off because they have not done that work themselves.

A more psychological understanding of this type of obsessive behavior and unhealthy competitiveness could be viewed through the concept of "goodness". If you believe, see, and value *your* own goodness, you can also recognize goodness more readily in others. Yet what if you do not value or see the good that innately lives within you? A trusted expert recommended a quality book to me on this very subject. *Cinderella and Her Sisters: The Envy and*

The Envied, written by Ann and Barry Ulanov, "...explores the psychological and theological aspects of envy and goodness. From how feminine and masculine parts of persons fit or do not fit together, to how individuals conduct their lives with those of the same and opposite sexes, how they conflict, compete, or join harmoniously...The authors focus on the nature of goodness as it surfaces...They reflect on its abundance, ability to unite disparate parts, its abiding presence, and its joy, and conclude with a brief review of the psychological literature on envy."

I now hold no animosity towards her because I can also see how much she is struggling with her own inner stuff that has nothing to do with me – and it never did. Yet when we are on the receiving end of personal, damaging attacks, well, that sets up a whole other dynamic.

At times we are really pushed to stand stronger in our own selves and trust our own path no matter how other people are responding to that. Since this was an ongoing experience that lasted for multiple years, I certainly ebbed and flowed with my inner strength. Even when I crumbled, I rose back up and kept going because at the end of the day, I know who I am; I know what I am here to do; and I have work to do. *Keep going.*

I also found more peace with the understanding that she is the *archetype* of a certain female energy that I needed to experience in order to master it more fully. This archetype attacks out of the smaller places within her because there is a huge gap between her own sense of self-worth, self-love, and self-acceptance. I do not even think she is a horrible person. I believe she is a beautiful person who has some really deep level self-value stuff to heal — but that is none of my business, really.

You know you have deeply healed from something really hard and difficult when you experience emotional neutrality around it. When you can witness that person without any big emotional reaction or response then you have a clear signal it has been completed for you. That is priceless peace. When I accidentally see her on a television show, or in an online video, or something pops up on my social media, I simply think, "Hmmm. Cute shoes." Then I get back to my priorities.

As all of this clears out, there is one more thing I have realized. By the time the truth rises, whenever, or however, or if that happens, I will not even care anymore.

That is what the truth does for you spiritually and energetically: it sets you free from disillusions you do not want to connect with and then fortifies you even more at a core level.

Another friend recommended a book to me that helped ground me in the truth I want to embody. *Finite and Infinite Games* by James Carse brilliantly depicts two ways we can move through life, the grandest game of all, and consciously choose how we want to play with others:

"Finite games are the familiar contests of everyday life; they are played in order to be won, which is when they end. But infinite games are more mysterious. Their object is not winning, but ensuring the continuation of play. The rules may change, the boundaries may change, even the participants may change — as long as the game is never allowed to come to an end. Finite games may offer wealth and status, power and glory, but infinite games offer something far more subtle and far grander."

We can easily connect finite games with the drive of the ego, and infinite games with the spiritual quest. We may play finite games in some smaller areas of our life, but how do you want to play in the grand scheme of it all?

What is your driving truth in how you will suit up and show up to the ongoing game of life? My philosophy is that we all benefit from the ongoing continuation of spiritual knowledge and information, and there is nothing to be won in a spiritual sense. The purpose is to keep the game alive, to bring in more people, and to expand it out to support even more individuals on their path. None of us owns the game, and control is just an illusion. Power fades and status changes. She may have *New York Times* Bestselling Author credibility, but I am proud to carry a deeper truth that I hope lasts far, far longer than my temporary time on the planet.

Practicing and implementing our spiritual work is hard at times. Please know you are not alone in those periods of hardship and emotional intensity. We need to—have to—go through the layers of it. No shortcuts here, and you would not want them, anyways. Wherever there are shortcuts is where you have to go back and re-work something at some point. A lot of spiritual propaganda tells you to stay positive, practice affirmations, avoid negativity, and all that jazz -- please be careful which of those pills you swallow. The side effects can take you way off course. It all comes down to working with your own energy. In order to do that, you have to be honest and real with yourself without glossing over your own inner truth.

When we are conscious of what we feel and we can move through it with authenticity, we eventually come out on the other side with a huge stack of gorgeous gold nuggets. It is in our best good to take the higher path – and yet that can be a very lonely and quiet place. It can take a lot longer than you expect. Just one step at a time keeps you moving forward – and that is all you need to commit to at times. One step today. One step tomorrow.

And on it goes. *Inner unicorn!*

I am sharing this story now because it is energetically complete for me. I have grown and healed a ton from it. The emotional intensity has cleared out; it was heavy and now it is light. My intention is to offer this experience as an example of how our spiritual work and spiritual teachers show up in various forms.

When I was wounded, hurt, and discouraged, it was very hard to share my experience. Feeling powerless does that – it closes down your voice and your truth. Yet being on the other side of it now has brought me new levels of strength, determination, and pride in what I was moving through. There was a small glimmering light that I kept focusing on.

A deeper part of me hopes this experience helps more people clear this energy in their own lives, if they are moving through a similar dark time of being on the receiving end of obsessive targeting, professional bullying, or nasty attacks. Depending on your circumstances, it may be appropriate to take legal action or speak with a human resources professional in your workplace. Please do not let it sink in and live in your psyche for too long. Feel it. Talk with a trusted friend. Allow it to move through you with grace and emotion. These things affect us and it is okay to feel all of it. Then you will once again find the strength to carry on and continue YOUR conversation with God. Neale Donald Walsh wrote a book on this topic that may help you get clear around exactly what you want that ongoing dialogue to be with Source.

No one can take away your energy, your purpose, mission, work, or energetic awesomeness, no matter how they are acting in their human suit. They are also God in human form. If you can find that part of them, you'll find more peace in yourself and throughout the process. We each have relationships with God to work through. When it is unconscious, it reveals itself in lower energies, darkness, and untruths.

You will have also changed your own energy when you carry that small piece of it in your pocket. Changing your own energy shifts it all.

When it is over, remember to take the best, leave the rest, and know that very little of it really matters once you are on the other side. But some of the best stuff — the growing stuff — comes up in the yucky middle. How you move through it on a daily basis will matter most to your heart, sense of self, and personal integrity. Stay in those places as best you can. And never doubt what a good cry, shout, and laugh can do to heal you up real good.

One of my favorite passages is called *The Paradoxical Commandments* and it was written by Dr. Kent M. Keith. This version below has been erroneously attributed to Mother Teresa because she had it hanging in one of Calcutta orphanages, yet Dr. Keith is the rightful author.

May it be of inspiration and a powerful torch of truth for you as the infinite game moves on.

> *"People are often unreasonable, illogical, and self-centered. Forgive them anyway.*
>
> *If you are kind, people may accuse you of selfish motives. Be kind anyway.*
>
> *If you are successful, you will win some false friends and true enemies. Succeed anyway.*
>
> *Honesty and frankness make you vulnerable. Be honest and frank anyway.*
>
> *The biggest men and women with the biggest ideas can be shot down by the smallest men and women with the smallest minds. Think big anyway.*

People favor underdogs, but follow only top dogs. Fight for a few underdogs anyway.

What you spend years building, someone could destroy overnight. Build anyway.

If you find serenity and happiness, they may be jealous. Be happy anyway.

The good you do today, people will often forget tomorrow. Do good anyway.

Give the world the best you have and it may never be enough. Give them your best anyway."

**~ "The Paradoxical Commandments"
by Dr. Kent M. Keith**

~

OWNING ALL OF YOUR ENERGY

A FTER HE WAS ENLIGHTENED, Buddha, also known as the Blessed One, was walking along a road in India when a brahman saw him walking by. The brahman, a member of the priest caste, noticed that this walking man was shining and glowing beyond anything else he had witnessed before. The brahman looked down at the muddy road where he was walking and saw something unusual: this man's footprints were in the shapes of wheels with spokes and rims. These were not the footprints of a mere human being.

The brahman watched as the walking man left the road and went to sit under a nearby tree, presumably to get out of the sun's intense rays. The brahman followed him to his resting place, and with great respect, approached the sitting man. Then he asked, "Master, you are glowing and your footprints are not those of a human beings. Are you a deva *(a god)*?"

"No, brahman, I am not a deva," replied the man sitting under the tree.

"Master, are you a reincarnation of god?"

"No, brahman, I am not."

"Master, are you a wizard or a magician?"

"No, brahman, I am not."

"Master, are you a human being?"

"No, brahman, I am not."

Puzzled, the brahman asked, "Then Master, what are you?"

"I am awake," replied Buddha.

When Buddha had previously sat under the Bodhi tree and experienced nirvana – the ability to tap into *no thing* or *being unbound*—he became enlightened to the purpose of life. Buddha awakened to his energetic state of not being one thing, but of being connected to all things. The understanding of his own light and presence in the Universe, and being of the Universe, was the foundation for his teachings on being awake, as well as the Four Noble Truths that he taught to those who came to him for guidance. Buddha's energy field changed because of the truth he connected to: all of his energy was all of the Universe. This popular tale is an excellent example of how to be all of your energy, all of your light, and simply walk in the world with it.

Understanding energetic signatures and the "language" of what cannot be seen is a new frontier for mass consciousness. To serve the expansion of consciousness, groups of souls chose to work with energy exploration further by embodying high-vibrational ways of giving and receiving energy frequencies. This soul choice can show up in the form of being an empath, intuitive, psychic, highly-sensitive person, lightworker, and/or intuitively working with the senses: clairaudient (hearing), clairsentient (feeling), clairvoyant (seeing), clairalience (smelling), claircognizance (knowing), and clairgustance (tasting).

If you possess one, or any combination, of these skills, you are connected to a soul group of millions who intend to guide humans towards their full multi-sensory potential. The good news is that everyone has access to these talents. Everyone on the planet has intuitive guidance and the ability to develop higher senses. Yet understanding the power and gifts of energy is an incredible tool that most of society does not know how to appreciate yet. If you already possess these traits, you are a pioneer in this field. And these talents will continue to evolve as millions awaken to their innate spiritual gifts and energy potentials.

The ability to feel energy shifts is becoming a normal, everyday experience for millions of people. If you look at the timeline of human evolution, this is a relatively new phenomenon — and it beautifully demonstrates humanity's growth. Energy has always existed in everything, but the increased understanding of spiritual energy in modern civilization is relatively new.

The greatest on-going obstacle to understanding energy dynamics will be the mind's desire for proof and validation. The ego will require this demonstration of value as well, so you will need to continually practice trusting what you cannot see or prove. Trust what you feel. Requiring proof is valid for many situations, but in the instance of energy, needing proof is actually an expression of density. Anything you can see or touch has a lower density than what you can feel. Many spiritual seekers have an elevated ability to feel and sense information as a signature of higher vibration multi-sensory talents.

Intuitive feeling is a higher frequency than the visual world's frequency. From an evolutionary standpoint, the most sensitive species were the ones who survived the longest because they could sense danger ahead of time. Their developed skills allowed them to sense when something was amiss, or different, or potentially threatening. They could run for cover or hide for protection. They could clear out before the pack of wolves found them. But now it is time to turn this "feel or flight" response around because you're not in survival situations anymore. You can relax into your feelings. You are a fully present, gorgeous being of energy. Embrace your feeling territory and own it with power.

Oftentimes, spiritual seekers cover up their energy gifts with guilt, denial, shame, pain, or hurt. Many have been shamed or ridiculed for being "too sensitive." Many of you have had lifetimes of spiritual persecution for what they knew, or did, or taught. A number of ancient mystery schools attempted to keep sacred practices hidden because the outer world was not a safe place to expose these abilities. You will be required to work through any lower vibrations you may hold about yourself and your talents.

Many individuals absorbed these perspectives of being "less than" or "too sensitive" as factual demonstrations of their self-worth. You absorbed the energy of being outcasts, different, not belonging, feeling small, and ultimately, not lovable. These messages created a very real wound. It is a very hurtful experience to be made fun of, or dismissed, or denied, or excluded, or rejected for being yourself. And for decades, there has been little supportive information about how to heal this part of yourself, or even a recognition that it has been damaging to your self-worth. If this has been a theme in your life, know that this experience also holds your greatest healing potential and gifts.

Now is the time to turn this perspective around. You can transmute it into greater self-acceptance. You must see yourself as gifted, strong, talented, and alive with spirit. You can explore why you, as a soul, chose to have the experience of being an outcast and how that has ultimately served you in being stronger, more loving, more kind. You are responsible for removing any victim consciousness energy you may hold about your self-identity, and ask yourself empowering questions that serve your commitment to self-love. Denying any of these parts of yourself is denying your truth.

You, as a soul, chose to come in with certain talents — and you knew it would be hard at times because you would be different. But you said you would do it anyway because you knew the perceived hardships would be temporary, and you would arrive on the other side with greater strength and love for yourself. From this perspective, it is not even logical to work against yourself in any way or to hold any victim consciousness energy. You knew you would emerge with new levels of love.

Now it is time to love all parts of yourself that you doubted, or discounted, or ignored. Now is the time to embrace the fullness of your gifts and how you stand out in the crowd. Now is the time to upgrade all lower perceptions of yourself into the highest possible realms. You are a leader of the new energies. Claim all parts of your self-identity with deep self-respect and solid confidence.

The world needs new frequencies more than ever. It is not always easy to be an energetic leader, the one who is different, but you are being given a conscious choice to love yourself more. That is all you must do. Turn the story around and see how your energy has served you in amazing ways. You can reprogram yourself to look at each prior wounding experience from a higher understanding of self-love.

One effective method to actively practice this reprogramming is to develop strong phrases you feel comfortable speaking the next time you are in a situation where someone calls you "too sensitive," or disrespects your abilities, or takes a dig at your energy skills, or insults your individuality. It is as simple as saying "thank you" to another person, even if they are being insulting. You do not need to meet them in that energy.

Instead, you can raise the vibration by communicating gratitude:

"Yes, I have been gifted with sensitivity and it has served me well in my life."

"Thank you for noticing one of my talents."

"My sensitive qualities have given me huge amounts of strength. I am quite grateful for this part of my identity."

"Thank you. I collect a lot of valuable information about people through all of my senses."

"I love this quality in myself. It adds a lot to my life experiences."

You can choose to respond from a high-vibrational place even amongst low-vibrational energies. When you express gratitude for your gifts, you immediately change the energy and call in greater self-respect, integrity, and Self-love. Each time you stand strong in your gifts, you elevate the frequency around you and develop new conscious thoughts about your own worthiness.

Consider your high-vibrational talents in another way. You may be "the sensitive one" in the group, in your family, or in a workplace, but this also means you are collecting more information than other people. You are collecting more insights about a situation that others are not connecting with or tuning into. You are picking up on what is below the surface, or another's true feelings, or unexpressed needs. You are collecting a more holistic picture of all energies that are in play.

It is a supreme gift to be aware of your multi-sensory

abilities and how this ability to collect information serves you. You have access to higher states of energy that support you, and ultimately, everyone else, in perfect ways. Trust what you feel and use that information with the best of intentions.

As you expand on your journey, you will find yourself placed in situations that allow you to develop and practice more self-love. You will feel stronger because of these circumstances. If needed, imagine your spiritual team and angels standing right next to you in their full power and presence. Know that you are supported and loved for being a high-vibrational person. The world needs you, even if they do not know it yet.

When you open up to higher frequencies of love, you will feel it rush in to guide you forward as part of your truth. You will find yourself in circumstances, conversations, and interactions that you will instantly recognize as an opportunity to demonstrate love-based truth verbally and energetically.

Unconditionally loving yourself is an integral part of your lifetime journey. You will find yourself in relationships, situations, and experiences that reflect this love back to you, and you will discern more quickly when there is not a vibrational match. You will be okay with transitions and change knowing that all is happening for the greatest good of all. You will have fewer attachments to specific outcomes. You will remove unconscious expectations of other people to be a certain way. An inner peace will gracefully carry you in all areas of your life.

Prepare for continual openings to more love as you stay open to finding it. There is no end to these energies unless you shut them down, block them, or constrict yourself. And if you do, for whatever reasons, you can always open back up to them. They are waiting for you at all times, in all ways, in all places, and the connection is eternal. You are these vibrations even when your temporary reality says you are separate in some way.

As your truth grows in connection to unconditional love, you will become your own best friend. You will speak to yourself as a most cherished friend would, and provide yourself with ongoing support, recognition, and kindness. You will feel like a full and complete vessel who is doing the best they can every day, in all ways. Compassion and self-forgiveness will guide you through sticky situations, and your intuition will increase as you value yourself more. You will naturally desire to connect with others who hold this same vibration of Self-love and personal acceptance. Everything shifts for the better when you shift to a higher version of yourself.

One way to actively practice more love in our modern era is through your social media channels. Only allow positive, uplifting information to reach you in your news feeds, within groups, and in communities. Be selective about whom you connect with regularly. Be mindful of where your energy levels rise and fall: Do I feel excited and happy in this space, or is my energy starting to sink? Do I genuinely enjoy these people or do I feel an obligation that weighs me down? Is this the best use of my time and energy right now, or would I rather be doing something else?

Take control of your social media interactions as a representation of your truth. Honor your newsfeeds as a reflection of how you honor your personal space. Would you want this interaction, group, or message in your living room? Social media is a wonderful opportunity to honor your boundaries and energy levels. Filter your newsfeeds with the tools provided through each social media channel (lists, groups, blocking, privacy settings, etc.) to reinforce what is best for your energy needs. Own it every time you scroll and skim.

Another way to practice honoring your truth regularly is through your social commitments. When you connect with friends, social groups, and acquaintances, check in with your energy levels before, during, and after each interaction. Watch how you feel within these connections. Based on the information you discern, continue to commit to the people and groups that raise your energy. If you spend 60% of your time with energy-raising individuals, these interactions will compensate for the 40% of your time you must spend with lower vibrational people. You have choice in how you spend your energy and with whom you personally connect with in your life. Consciously own this choice and make necessary changes. Watch as your energy rises over time.

As you shift to operating from a new place of truth, you may experience relationship changes with friends, groups, acquaintances, colleagues, and family members. This is highly normal during this time, and ultimately, it was planned on a soul level. You have served those whom you no longer have a connection with, and they have served you. Now you are both free to go forward on your paths and make new vibrational matches with like-minded souls. What a perfect Universal system that allows both parties to continue on their best possible paths.

The journey of unconditionally loving yourself is a gift from your soul. After lifetimes of learning, karma, healing, and lower vibrational experiences, you are now ready to receive the full celebration of your light. You are blossoming and opening up to more of your innate energy of pure joy. You are here to be love in human form and to follow the bliss of your energy.

The energy you exude changes as you awaken to more of yourself as unconditional love.

Unconditionally loving yourself more becomes a guiding truth that irrevocably changes your life experience and inner world.

~~

THEN SOMETHING AMAZING
HAPPENED AT A PARTY

WARM AIR SOFTENED MY FROZEN face as we pushed inside, away from the cold, icy wind. The shock of heat was inviting and relaxing; my shoulders dropped two inches with relief. A quartet of musicians jammed along in the background as we removed our coats, gloves, and scarves, shaking off the frigid winter temps and moving further away from the entrance. More people poured in through the swinging doors right behind us, looking for food, fun, and a great celebration. Laughter echoed around the interior; two children ran by holding raffle tickets.

Hand in hand, my husband and I followed the winding heads as they moved towards the heart of the party. The professional photographer pulled us into his click, click, click range as we smiled and quickly posed for photos we would never see. Instinctively, we moved towards the crowded bar to gather our first round of drinks. The bartenders were in frantic motion, the most popular people at the party, and a stark contrast to the jam-packed stationary bodies waiting patiently, eagerly, for a smooth dark red or frothy pale yellow drink.

Glasses in hand, and finally feeling warmer, we slowly made the rounds to greet friends and co-workers, meet new faces, shake cold hands, and glance at people who looked vaguely familiar. A few people congratulated us on our recent wedding, occurring only months ago, and asked us about upcoming honeymoon plans. Talk, talk, listen, listen, laugh, laugh. Then the soundtrack quietly changed to growl, growl, growl as my stomach demanded attention.

The evening's food buffet was in yet another big room, which opened up to more laughter and whiffs of grilled salmon and spicy chicken. We navigated sideways through people balancing plates with wine glasses and small circles of conversations. Thirty minutes later, we had shrimp, seasoned potatoes, teriyaki chicken, and veggies piled up high on very tiny plates. It was standing room only to eat, yet thankfully I found a spot in a corner, away from wild elbows and potential plate disasters. A brief respite from the chaos. A moment to eat and breathe.

"Do you think he is here tonight?" I have been peering around the party all night, looking for the famous face in the crowd.

"Probably." My husband replied, teriyaki chicken disappearing.

"I guess the odds of meeting him are slim, but an author can hope, right?"

He half smiled. "I bet we'll see him. I'm sure he would come tonight."

I nodded in agreement. "I just want to tell him thank you because... he changed my life. He allowed me to make my dreams come true, ya know?" Wine glass almost empty.

Another knowing nod. Oh yes, my husband knows. I have not been able to stop talking about the possibility of meeting this famous man. It was not likely, but it was probable so I remained hopeful. Fingers crossed.

Our plates were emptied rather quickly, but unfortunately the food line was too long to load up again. There was another option to pursue, though, if most people were in line for the buffet.

"Let's get *another* drink before we go down to the presentation."

Hand in hand, and using his gift of height, he steered us sideways through more voices, shoulders, and laughter. Music played on, upbeat and celebratory, until the roaming crowd was invited to move downstairs for the evening's next event. We shuffled along slowly as I reviewed how big this year had been.

Six months earlier, I did it. I finally published my first book. Four years after being shut down by that literary agent, and many publishing rejections, and moving through the struggle and silence, I kicked myself forward with a grander truth that felt so right. The belief that I had something to say that could help people – inspire them, heal them, benefit them – became too strong to ignore. Even if I was wrong, and it led nowhere, I had to try. I realized you can only walk through IKEA and admire the bright lights so many times until you have to take ownership of your own light. Would I hate myself for not even attempting?

Yes.

The truth within me rose up. I can still clearly remember that one Saturday morning when I woke up and something had switched inside of me. New inspirations for the book came bolting through me and a fresh writing approach was exploding with ideas. I grabbed my laptop and sat down on the couch to write, write, write before the inspirations fluttered out the window. I did not even stand up from the couch until later in the afternoon when I realized I should probably eat something.

Four months after that, I had completely rewritten the book and hit publish on Amazon. My book was live. *Now published.* I was ecstatic, perplexed, and absolutely terrified, all at the same time. I went for a long, long walk to move the energies through me. I was finally an author. And it was because of one man in particular who gave me everything I needed to make that dream a reality.

After the presentation ended, the lights were turned back up and we slowly made our way to the front of the room. Shoulders to shoulders, moving slowly through the crowd, I could faintly see his head. More walking space started to open up as people surged back to the bar and dessert tables. The man I wished to thank was right there. *Right there.* Of course, he was surrounded by incoming people asking for autographs and others stopping to shake his hand. The odds were very slim that I could make contact, but maybe it would happen. He could turn and leave at any moment. We shuffled forward.

He was only ten feet away. His laugh was loud and gregarious and open; the kind that makes you want to laugh along with him and be in on the joke. Butterflies began dancing within; their wings fluttered awake at an instinctual level. *Just be normal.*

Five feet away. Titans of industry often seem larger than life because of their world status, innovative influence, and life-changing businesses. They are the world elite, topping important global lists, constantly on the move in private planes, and secreted away in important meetings; untouchable and mysterious. Until they are no longer a face on the cover of a magazine, but someone who was actually standing right in front of you. *He is a normal human being. Just be cool.*

Two feet away. We moved forward, my hand

grasping my husband's hand so tightly he stopped to turn back and gave me a look. *Deep breaths. Just speak like a normal person.*

One foot away. *Butterflies, butterflies, butterflies.*

He was right there. We were standing to his left as another person ended a conversation and walked away. Then he turned to look at us and smiled.

"Hi there, how are you this evening?" His voice was warm, hand extended in a handshake to my husband.

"We're doing well, thank you. I know you have a lot going on and we don't want to take up your time, but I wanted to introduce you to Molly."

And then I was shaking hands with Jeff Bezos.

"Hi Molly, it's nice to meet you. Are you enjoying the party?"

"Absolutely, it's lovely. I just wanted to come up and personally thank you for Kindle. I am an author, and it is a platform that literally allowed me to make my dreams come true. So thank you very much."

Big smile from Mr. Bezos. "The Kindle team is killing it and they are doing a phenomenal job. What is your book about?"

"It's a travel memoir, and it actually made it to the Kindle Top 100 earlier this month, I couldn't believe it."

"Well congratulations. That is great. It's fantastic to see how Kindle has grown. Good luck with your next book."

"Thank you, I appreciate it."

He smiled. I smiled. Then we walked away as another person engaged him in conversation.

My head was spinning. This is what it must feel like for a software engineer to meet Bill Gates, or a graphic designer to have met Steve Jobs.

As we moved back into the energy of the party, I

swear I heard a cosmic giggle, a gentle confirmation that sometimes you do not have to follow the path that everyone else takes. You do not have to give up on a dream. You do not have to let anything take you away from what you believe is your truth or what you can contribute back to the world. Even when you want to give up, come back to that pure truth that is burning and surging within you that perhaps it is something bigger than you in the first place. Perhaps that dream you are feeling, that is calling you persistently, is not even about you at all. Perhaps that flame is connected to a grander source of energy that is meant to be expressed in a way only you can do so.

These are the realizations that shifted me away from thinking about the dream of writing a book to actively creating it. These are the understandings I arrived at as part of my own inner truth. I reached a point where I did not need anyone else to agree with what I knew was true for me. I just needed to agree strongly with myself, and let that inner alignment be enough.

Let your own truth make you full and feel nourished.

Back in 2009, I temporarily gave my personal truth away to that literary agent's truth. I gave my power away to her expertise, so I finally called it back and steered myself to a deeper truth. I am going to follow this dream, even if it tanks, even if I never write another book again, even if it is harder than I expect, because this creative expression is the truth of who I am right now. I will do it knowing that it can potentially support and help other people. Millions of people around the globe are following their dreams every day.

Why not you, too? Why would you hold back who you are…for anything?

We have to hold ourselves accountable for believing

in ourselves.

We have to hold ourselves to a higher standard of inner knowingness that lights the way, glows from within, and shines out with faith on an unknown path.

We have to own those parts of ourselves that want to hide, or disappear, or stay small. We have to let those inner messages express themselves.

We have to let them rise.

YOUR TRUTH AS AN INNER FORTRESS

AS THE SUN GRADUALLY APPEARS over the horizon, its soft mango rays returning in full force, an impressive stone fortress receives the warmth of this fresh light. Atop rolling hills, trees sway in the morning breeze and leaves dance down to the ground. A river flows closer into view, meandering across an open field, and eventually connects to a moat circling around the fortress walls. The water moves briskly as strong gusts of wind blow through; waves lap up against the stone bricks and splash onto the cold wall. Patches of moss grow in between the brick cracks, hidden from the sun's view.

A drawbridge, currently closed, stands thirty feet high at the front entrance. When it is slowly cranked down, a whole inner world of activity is revealed: music, community, dancing, creativity, celebration, and family. When it is closed, tightly pressed to the wall's strength, there is barely a sound to be heard about the inner workings of the fortress.

Arched windows, many with stained glass mosaics, dot the walls with dancing colors and gorgeous stories depicting the life and times of this powerful structure. The key moments that have created this place are held in high regard as honored events and sacred memories. They have literally formed the bones of this fortress.

Glancing up higher, turrets adorn the tops of the walls with tall towers in each corner. Torches of light sit at each peak. These burning flames continue to surge through every storm and moonless night, rarely ever extinguished for long. From a distance, these blazing fires light up the whole countryside for miles and miles.

This is no ordinary fortress sitting on a gorgeous property somewhere, collecting dust bunnies and turning into a dilapidated Airbnb rental. This stone fortress, ancient yet timeless, is meant to be a strong visual of your truth. It is a monumental structure built on a foundation of faith and designed to last through storms, wars, and the aging of life. No matter what passes by outside those four walls, there is a realm of safety and strength that permeates through all of life's ongoing events and experiences.

The many bricks that compose the fortress represent your belief system. Each brick is an important occasion or formative memory. Your values, beliefs, views, opinions, and what you find meaningful are all stacked here, creating the exterior of the structure and determining how you want to experience your terrain of truth.

The stained glass windows in the fortress walls are the stories you share and tell the world. They showcase what you create and put out for others to understand based on what you cherish and what has value to you. The meaning and numerous memories of your life are brought to visual depiction in these creations so others can know you and see you in all your colorful splendor.

The grand entrance to this amazing place is the drawbridge, which ultimately reveals your choice points. What will you allow into your energy field and inner space? What will be granted permission to enter? Or when will you drop the drawbridge down to allow your needs, your voice, and your full self to shine out? As you become more skilled at discerning who arrives at the front door, you will be more adept at making choices that are in the best possible alignment for you.

It may seem that your mind or ego would be good commanders of this drawbridge post, as they have the intellect and might to guard the gates. But over time, it is likely that you have found the best commander of the drawbridge is actually your heart, working alongside your mind and ego. Your heart probably has many interesting stories of its own to tell about being held in the dungeon of this fortress, or perhaps being exiled and stranded outside the walls. Your heart knows every story in the stained glass windows, as well as the foundation that the fortress has been built upon. As you have connected with more of your relentless truth, and what is essential to your life, it has made more sense to continually follow your heart's guidance and advice. Your heart is the High Commander of the drawbridge, sitting up in the highest guard tower, and giving orders to all. Your heart, mind, and ego together determine your choice points and what is best for your life. This trifecta runs the gates, holds the controls, and wields power as needed.

And when someone or something is denied entry to the fortress? Well, down to the moat they go! The shallow stream captures all of their feelings, emotions, and energies that you do not want to accept. The moat provides a kind place for their energies to splash-land – no drowning or crocodiles, unless that is what you prefer – and is a gentle way for all of that undesirable stuff to float away, down the river, off into the horizon.

Ultimately, nothing penetrates this fortress. No

traveling idiots, no passing fools, no lost competitive bitches, no dream-denying agents, no crazy maniacs, and no Trojan horses. Inside the fortress, there is much activity, fun, and joy to embrace! All of your energy is living, creating, and dancing in beautiful safety and glee. You can look up at the stained glass windows and smile at all of the wonderful times that have created such a glorious place to call your own.

When there were ego deaths, you rebuilt with stronger bricks. When you found a section of weakness in your personal belief system, you had everything you needed to strengthen and upgrade what called to you next. When you no longer needed to hold back your light, everything that was not truly you was taken away by the forces of the winds and the ease of angel wings.

Inside the fortress walls, your truth reigns supreme through unconditional love. Truth sits with you in an empty car, steers you through the IKEA aisles (yes, there is an IKEA inside this fortress, just go with it), and guides you to trust, trust, trust what you are feeling at a deeper level of your being. Truth embraces rejections as a test of unconditional acceptance and loves you bigger than judgment. Truth wraps you up with more unconditional love.

Truth reminds you to keep making strong choices that enhance your sense of power and purpose. Truth sits with you through the tough emotions so you can hear the truest messages within yourself. Truth gives you strength to share your energy with the right people who see you and respect you. Truth asks you to think bigger about the possibilities for your life and to trust the creative sparks that call to you. Truth says you can do whatever creatively inspires you simply because you dreamed it. Truth keeps you going despite anything that is happening inside, or outside, of its walls.

You feel all of this innately. You know it to be true at the deepest levels of your being. When you felt temporary doubt or discouragement, an inner burning fire kept pushing you forward during the learning curves and periods of uncertainty. The blazing torch keeps persisting even when creative confidence deflates or bigger possibilities are unclear. You feel protected and strong because you are grounded in deep roots of faith.

As you climb up to one of the high towers, and look out at the amazing view from atop this fortress, you can see the beauty of everything. You feel connected to everything. You recognize truth within yourself. Then you see how truth is everything, everywhere, always.

You see the open field of wildflowers brimming with possibilities and new roads to follow.

You watch as the flower stems fold and bend in the wind, and then they rise again.

You know that tree roots venture down into the soil for stability, and then the tree rises.

You witness a tree release dead leaves, so a truer and healthier expression will rise.

You observe how a bird lands, walks, and pecks, but ultimately the bird is made to rise up again.

As the moon rises high, and then slides back down to the ground, weary from a night of splendor, you know it will reliably rise again tomorrow.

From this perspective, you can see how everything in the natural world is made to descend and then rise again. The same incredible forces that move the sun, the moon, the trees, and the energies of life move through you in concert with the grand scheme of the Universe. You are a timeless element of unconditional love amongst the chaos and perfection of the Universe, amplifying the truth of your soul in human form for a temporary visit. The passing leaves, the falling bricks, the flowing water, and the tireless flames mean nothing in the long run because it is the truth of something far grander that is guiding you forward.

No matter what dark passage you must walk through, or if you are temporarily stuck in a dungeon of your own making, or you are trudging through endless dark caves, banging your head against unrelenting walls, you now carry a greater light inside that reminds you this is all temporary. This all changes, anyways. You are making a fleeting stop on a much longer journey that is truly about creating more unconditional love in yourself and in the Universe.

And you will continue to rise.

REFERENCES
AND
RECOMMENDED RESOURCES

Carse, James. *Finite and Infinite Games: A Vision of Life as Play and Possibility*. Originally published in 1986. Free Press, Simon and Schuster, 2011.

Keith, Kent M. *Anyway: The Paradoxical Commandments. Finding Personal Meaning In A Crazy World*. Berkley, Reprint Edition 2004.

Ponder, Catherine. *Open Your Mind To Receive*. DeVorss and Company. 2007.

Sawyer, Irma Kaye. *The BrightStar Empowerments: Compilation Guide*. 2016.

Scovel Shinn, Florence. *The Game of Life and How To Play It*. Public domain. Originally published in 1925.

Ulanov, Ann and Barry. *Cinderella and Her Sisters: The Envy and the Envied*, Daimon Verlag, Updated Version, 2012.

Walsh, Neale Donald. *Conversations With God: An Uncommon Dialogue, Book 1,* TarcherPerigree, Penguin Group, First Edition, 1996.

"Dona Sutta: With Dona" (AN 4.36), translated from the Pali by Thanissaro Bhikkhu. *Access to Insight (BCBS Edition),* November 2013.

ح

ABOUT MOLLY McCORD

MOLLY McCORD, M.A., is a bestselling author, business coach for conscious entrepreneurs, intuitive astrologer, radio show host, and modern consciousness teacher.

She has published twelve books, created numerous online programs (summits, webinars, courses), hosted a weekly podcast with over 120,000 downloads, and advised numerous entrepreneurs and small business owners worldwide to better results. As a one-on-one coach, Molly has worked with hundreds of clients in 20 countries to know themselves and their purpose more fully at www.MollyMcCord.online.

Since 2013, over 50,000 copies of Molly's books have been downloaded globally. Her debut memoir, THE ART OF TRAPEZE: ONE WOMAN'S JOURNEY OF SOARING, SURRENDERING, AND AWAKENING, hit #1 in 2 Amazon categories within 3 days and hitting #6 worldwide in the Kindle Top 100.

Her latest publishing project, *Modern Heroine Soul Stories*, features 24 contributing authors in a special inspiring book with all proceeds being donated to the non-profit, Women for Women International.

Molly has a B.A. in Political Science and Women's Studies, and a Master's degree in International Relations and Diplomacy as a formal channel for understanding Global Consciousness with a Jungian perspective. Molly is currently an Ambassador for Women for Women International, a non-profit organization which provides education and business training for marginalized women in developing countries.

She resides in Florida with her husband and young son.

All of Molly's published books can be found at: www.Amazon.com/author/MollyMcCord

Connect with more of Molly's spiritual teachings at: www.ConsciousCoolChic.com

FREE CHAPTER EXCERPT

The Art of Trapeze:
One Woman's Journey of Soaring, Surrendering, and
Awakening

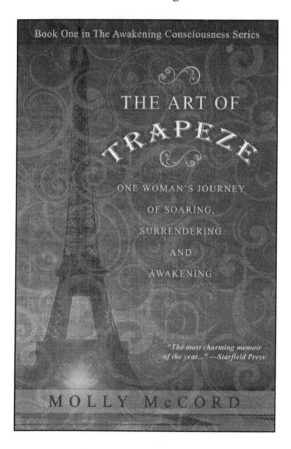

THE BIGGEST LAUNCH

THE SECRET TO JUMPING OFF a ridiculously high platform starts in the toes. All ten instinctively clench desperately to the cold steel slab's edge, insisting on a temporary delay until the timing is *just right*. Toes can be demanding and dramatic like that since they spend a whole lifetime rarely being seen and feel easily taken for granted. They tighten quickly and remain that way until I remember to give them adequate love; then they relaxed just enough to be my little supportive friends, but only until my focus goes somewhere else. Like over the front of this platform and into the grand abyss that fills the air in front of me. I squint my eyes to see something, anything out there, but nothing is in sight except a vast ocean of faint possibilities and foggy movements of distant clouds. All ten toes freeze up again.

So I turned my attention up, up, up to my fingers as they firmly grasped onto this tough wood bar that suddenly felt too weak. My chalked palms were satin and sticky, the perfect combination for touching this rung with commitment and agility. I loosened my wrists a bit and remembered to just let them hang, like limp noodles dangling from a slotted spoon. I tried not to blame the fingers for being tight since it was important that *they* gripped on well. It was most likely tension sent up directly from the toes as pleas of *Don't forget we need attention, too!*

A soft flurry of air tousled my long caramel hair that was held back in a ponytail; a loose strand escaped and inconveniently stuck itself to my glossed lips. The air was cooling and created goose bumps up my arms and down my spine. I could feel the tension gathering in my buttocks, unconsciously clenching and releasing to reaffirm control. I breathed in to loosen up my stomach muscles, or, more accurately the place where stomach muscles were supposed to be. (Blame the croissants.) My head briefly swayed in all directions on my neck like a bobble-head doll, twisting and moving to release any hidden tension.

Breathe.

Here I stood, once again prepared for a life-changing jump into the unknown. Breathe.

I had never been to Paris before. I did not have previous experiences of strolling along the Seine, or recollections of a romantic night in Montmartre, or a box of sepia-toned photos of myself standing in front of the Eiffel Tower in the sun, or Notre Dame in the rain, or even a still-life photo of a glorious *cafe au lait.* But in my typical brazen fashion, I was going out into the great unknown and moving to Paris. I knew I could make this incredible dream a reality. I could feel it as it pulled at my heartstrings and opened me up to a bigger life path. I barely spoke the language, I knew no one in the country, and I had no idea where I was going to live. But the details would come together once I arrived and got some grounding. Yes, definitely. Just breathe.

Everything was going to be amazing. Or it better be. Or I hoped it would be. Or it wouldn't be and this was going to fail and I'd fall again and…

Stop it. Breathe. Think happy thoughts. I turned my focus to how I had arrived at this life platform again and made this choice with my heart. I closed my eyes as the breeze kicked up my hair and my whole face started to smile, hair still stuck in glossy lips. It was four years ago when I had an unexpected date with my destiny.

I had moved back to Seattle after a year in Portland as a personal banker *(hated it, bored, tired of the sales goals and being nice to the obnoxious public*). The hot, rented U-haul pulled into my mom's driveway the first week of September 2001. Within weeks, the economy crashed due to the horror in New York City; my stand-by job possibilities disappeared overnight. A few weeks were spent on the couch and then I went to a job placement agency out of desperation. The wide woman in a clingy red shirt reported that she did not have any suitable job interviews to send me on at that time, and my heart sank with silent terror. But after a quick reach to another side of her desk, she opened a different colored file and said she could offer me a position as a Career Counselor due to my experience at the bank. I said yes, and obediently followed the training and protocol *(hated it, bored, tired of the sales goals and being nice to the obnoxious public)*. The office became increasingly uncomfortable as I shared a cubicle farm with five manipulative women who were always out for the most placements, the highest numbers, the top managerial recognition. I could be that intense too, I reasoned; I just didn't see that daily routine as something worth fighting for.

After four months of *really giving it my all*, I sat down with the manager in a private conference room right before lunch on a Tuesday. "There are a lot of things I am good at, but this job is not one of them. I need to move on and today is my last day. Maybe we have a job in the job binder I could interview for?" Her eyes lit up with lusty dollar signs about the commission she could earn on my job placement.

On a Tuesday morning exactly one week later, I accepted a job as a Marketing Coordinator for a small company that imported French products. It also turned out to be the same day I was meeting with a psychic lady as a gift from a family member to help me find clarity about my life direction. I was nervous and skeptical about the appointment since I had no idea what to expect or how these things worked. I was open to anything though, and if nothing else, it would be a good laugh.

I thought I had the wrong address when I pulled into the driveway of an old farmhouse, no flashing neon light in sight. I arrived an embarrassing twenty minutes late due to bumper-to-horn traffic and hoped she would not cancel the appointment. Or maybe I secretly hoped she would.

I sat down at a long wood table inside her studio office, three candles glowing away. "What's on your mind? What's coming up for you right now, kiddo?" She lifted a cup of hot tea to her lips and waited.

My instinct was to hold back a bit as I watched her with sideways eyes, waiting for a magic pouf, or magic crystal ball, or the air to fill with smoke. I moved my feet around under the table. Nope, no fog machine.

"I'm trying to figure out my career situation. What should I do with my life?"

Saying the words out loud made my stomach turn a little with dread and excitement, feeling both vulnerable and fearless in the same sentence. I was open to what I needed to do with my life; I just had no idea what that single magical thing was, like it was hidden from me but maybe accessible to her. She shook her thick wavy chocolate hair, eyes staring straight ahead, and said, "I see you in France."

I blinked. That was the most random thing ever and certainly not the career advice I was looking for. My brow started to furrow as I tried to fit the idea into my head and it had no place to go. I had never even been to Europe before, the continent of. My exotic international travel thus far included trips to the glorious shopping mecca of

Edmonton Mall in Alberta, Canada (*three Club Monaco stores in one place, this IS heaven!*), a few voyages north across the border into Vancouver, B.C. (as most Seattleites do), and a trip to Mazatlan once for spring break in college with a bunch of girlfriends. Oh gosh, I completely forgot, the funny story about going out to a beach club one night and dancing on top of the dirty wood table, the waves crashing twenty feet away, the music pounding, a packed dance floor, and... *me falling off the table* in front of everyone, high heels in the air, and...

Probably different cultural values in France.

"Huh," I replied, writing *live in France????* on my notepad. Then she asked if I had any connections to France, staring at me with a knowing expression and a slight smirk. My exhausted mind tried to fit some pieces together about who I knew that was French, or exotic, or maybe once brought me a souvenir from Paris. Anything, anyone?

"Oh wait. I started a new job today and they have a business connection to France." *Welcome to the topic, Molly.*

She lifted both eyebrows to the ceiling with a knowing smile. I stared at the notepad again. Me? In France? How in the world could that even happen? It sounded bizarre and unfeasible and yet incredibly awesome. I sat up straighter with intrigue and leaned in to the table, my necklace almost touching the wood surface.

"So, how do you see this fitting together? Me in France and all of... that?"

She shared the possible connections and ways things could unfold as I wrote feverishly, my brow still furrowed and overloaded with the information.

Then she paused and said, "You know, for only being 23, you have done a lot of personal development work that most women only start to look at in their forties."

I nodded silently, humbly, and wrote *a lot of self-work,* two stars. I absorbed the validation for the evenings I had spent sitting on my apartment floor figuring out which parts of myself I wanted to improve and which parts I adored. I had made lists of what I liked experiencing in relationships:

Weekend companionship

Holding hands without thinking about it

Sharing the TV couch comfortably

Trying new restaurants and ordering unpronounceable foods

Listening to all of my random thoughts

A continual collection of inside jokes

Someone else who will eat the leftovers so I don't feel guilty about throwing them away

Big feet and a big — (TO BE CONTINUED... red hearts);

I had another list going about what I wanted to experience on a daily basis: *Creativity, self-expression, supportive network, freedom to follow my energy and inspirations, financial stability, travel.* I felt a high every time I looked at this list with its bright, big letters. A smile would spread across my whole face and my body would start rocking a little.

As my conversation with this wise woman continued, I unexpectedly felt like this woman saw the hidden parts of me. Like my artistic talent that I let slip away years ago because I didn't think it was good enough for anyone to look at. Or the brief depression I went through in North Carolina and how it felt like a secret I could never, ever, *ever* reveal. Or the dissatisfaction I felt in Portland when I thought I should stay committed to a job I hated because it demonstrated that I was a real adult, making my way in the world, and therefore, it was important.

Maybe she saw all of this, maybe not. But something

within me started to both relax and open up. I slowly softened in my three-inch heels to the emerging possibility that it was okay to share those parts of me: the messy, the flaws, the insecurities, the doubts. It could be safe. It could be okay. I wrote *Open up more*, three stars, on the side of the paper. Underlined.

In only forty minutes, my life became bigger as the tiny unconscious self-imposed walls I was living within fell to the ground. *I could actually do exciting things in my life,* and dream a little bigger, and push beyond conventional options. And she reaffirmed that yes, (*yes, yes, yes*) there was definitely a plan for my life. My feet were pulsing with energy under the table.

But even more uplifting than the possibilities about the future was that I felt for the first time in my life *someone saw me*. ME. The ME I couldn't even see because I was wrapped up in confusion about my life direction and paying off my school debt and trying to figure out my career and wondering if I was missing out on something or someone. She saw more of ME than I could have ever imagined, including the spiritual talents I could develop. I didn't even realize I had never been seen like this before. My last scribbles were *Trust* and *Guided to set up what I need*, two stars each.

Afterward, I flew to my mom's house, the tires on my truck barely touching the ground. We pulled two chairs up to the kitchen table and I spilled everything about the session, diligently reviewing each line on my notepad, every single doodle, and trying to recall more tidbits. She nodded with huge smiles and excitement, putting her hand to her heart at just the right times and *getting it*.

Two years later, as desire for a new adventure grew, I went to Europe for the first time by myself. I arrived at the airport covered in black because based on all the fashion magazines I flipped through, black was obviously the standard attire of the chic French at all times, everywhere, always, no exceptions. I was going to be an instant local in my head-to-toe *noir*, no doubt about it, and blend into the French Alps region effortlessly while I was there studying French for five weeks. Except it turned out people traveling and living across the Atlantic *also* own jeans and bright cardigans and cute tunics with fun patterns and comfortable shoes. Who are these magazine writers, anyway? I looked like a one-person funeral procession walking down the gateway. I tried to maintain a too-cool-for-school vibe, but really I was terrified inside. I had no idea what life was like on another continent and my first piece of certain information was obviously wrong. I arrived in Geneva and during the shuttle ride to Annecy, France, I breathed in the invigorating mountain air and breathed out my fears. Over five short weeks, that trip opened up more of me and my life possibilities, and I loved being in France. How appropriate that I boarded the plane in funeral attire since a part of me did indeed die on that trip and a new version arrived back home. I returned to my life in America and felt uncomfortable because the environment no longer matched my heart. I needed to go back there. But I had no idea how, or when, or even why. It felt impossible and scary.

Until one random Thursday morning. I was at work, looking in the direction of my computer screen but not focused on it as my morning coffee grew colder to the right. The sun blazed warmly outside and briefly danced along the tops of my shoulders, but I felt my life force slowing, painfully leaking out of me. The energy sank down, down, down through my cushioned rolling faux leather chair, out of my three-inch heels, and into the thin gray office carpet. I slumped back, head on the chair, all zest officially gone. I looked at the calendar that said 2004. *This is how I'm spending my Thursday?* I had trained myself to feel excitement around the arrival of Fridays (*TGIF! See you at happy hour! What are your weekend plans?*), but that meant I was living life for one day a workweek and two weekend days. Less than fifty percent of a week. What would it be like to feel excited about *every* day? I picked up the mug of cold coffee and took a desperate sip to feel a jolt of life. Then I stood up and gave myself an early lunch break. I walked away from that stack of files and the marketing calendar and the red blinking voicemail light and the inbox staring back at me. I needed a new life.

In a nearby vacant park, I sat down with myself over a bright salad and remembered everything I had learned up to this point about my life choices. Making a choice and taking action on it was one thing; acting with Trust was a whole other declaration. Over the past two years, I had learned incredible wisdom from the psychic lady who became my unofficial spiritual teacher, counselor, and ongoing connection to All I Could Do In My Life. I had sessions with her a few times a year and arrived on time, even way too early, with a list of questions and an empty notepad. I learned about God, working with spiritual energy, detachment, getting out of my own way so something bigger and better could unfold. I was gifted with opportunities to apply these lessons in relationships, business, moving homes, and *getting clear about what I want*. She never told me what to do; I had to learn Trust for myself and listen to my own messages. And most of those Trust messages I let sit unanswered on the answering machine, silent blinking red lights that were available when I was ready. A true teacher will never give you the answers to the tests, but they will support you in figuring out the answers for yourself because that is how you connect with your own power. And I had learned that we were continually tested on these "things we know" as a way to demonstrate our evolving choices and intentions. So yes, I *knew* all about Trust, intentions, faith, and energy. I *knew* it was okay to dream bigger and Trust what I really wanted, but now it was time to act on it and make changes.

I never touched my salad during that "getting clear with myself" session.

I returned to the office with a click, click, click of my heels and a new strength in my posture. I pulled out the computer keyboard, and with chocolate-covered pretzels in hand, I typed "graduate schools in Paris."

The idea had been brewing for a while, but only as a safe daydream about how I could someday get on with my life and not be stuck with these commitments. It represented the day I would go for it, push the start button on my real life, go big. The *hows* had scared me for months because it felt too big, too complicated to figure out something as complex as moving to another country for a long time. How would I make money? How would I get a legal visa? How would I meet people? I had kept the possibility curbed and only thought about it when I had the emotional energy to dream.

Then that new beginning turned out to be this random Thursday. *The day* I was finally ready to Trust more. My mind was flying everywhere and the nerves were kicking in, but I exhaled and returned to Trust: in myself, in God, in the process, and in the possibilities I could not see. Now was the time to take the learning up, up, up to this higher platform of choice and do something with it even though it was incredibly exhilarating and scary in the same breath. Trust that God is right there, no matter what. Trust that it is safe to go for it, all of it. Trust that the Universe had my back.

And now that back—and fingers and heart and ten obnoxious toes—were all standing firm and strong on top of this highest of platforms. My previous trip to France was the stretch and warm up. Then I committed to this choice when I put my right foot and both hands on the bottom rungs of this ladder and applied for the student visa. And next I will soar on the moving bars and gain momentum to make this dream—this blooming part of Self—a flying declaration of Trust and the life I wanted. It was time to go for it, no holds barred. Well, except for the bar I held in my hands with my noodle wrists.

Tension began to creep slowly up my body again. *Shut up, toes. The ten of you do not have a majority vote.* Breathe.

The winds of possibility picked up even more. A breeze drifted across the right side of my body, and fifteen seconds later, I felt another breeze on my left side. I allowed both to carry away any lingering residual fears because, as I have learned through previous leaps, doubts, and uncertainties are simply too heavy to carry when the aim is to be Trust-full.

Instead, I had packed in my essence the skills and qualities I have been developing during all former soaring jumps. Solitude was strapped to my back and fortified my inner connections as a solo traveler. Endurance was molded to the bottom of both feet as a reminder to keep going, to stay focused, to follow the path as it presented itself. Strength was bound inside my core to provide comfort and security regardless of the external developments known as "life." Flexibility intermingled itself around both legs to keep them limber and poised, quick and adaptable. Style was nestled with flair in the back of my flowing hair, just out of sight from my green eyes. And Heart filled up my aura and provided a protective coating to keep me safe from my ego's desire to always, always, always lead, and reminded me to return to the present moment.

Breathe.

I did a deep knee bend to stretch all stiff leg joints, and as I was halfway down, hands still on the bar, I felt the dual urges to go forward courageously and the comfort of keeping my feet on this platform. It was normal to feel the push and pull between the Heart's openness and the ego's need to control during big change, so I had learned to expect it. But I also had a mantra readily available for these conflicting directions: Yes from the Heart and no from the Ego, but still go for it. "Yes and no, but still go."

As I straightened my spine and arched with subtle confidence, I felt adrenaline quicken in my stomach. Any minute now it would be time to go.

Ya hear that, toes? Get ready. They twitched and released in waves, up and down in rhythm.

My last intentional thought before every jump, with softly closed eyes, was to visualize angel wings. Hefty, weighted white feathers padded together so thickly they were dense with support and yet lighter than air, than dust, than the chalk on my hands. I pictured satin wings with hints of sparkles embedded deeply into every fine bristle. When the bristles blew in the wind, each one moved and flowed freely, but the feather's core remained erect and strong. They were a collection of comfort that demonstrated how soaring, jumping, and Trusting could be light and grace-filled. And these wings I envisioned reminded me that I was never alone as long as my heart was open wide and beating strong, filling my body with breath all the way down to my toes.

Time to let go, little piggies. Yes, we're doing this now. Together. My toes released and relaxed as I expanded my chest and inhaled deeply. A final flutter from unseen wings cooled off my face, my throat, my arms. And in less than a second, a force of powerful air rushed in to cover the front of my body as I jumped into the oblivion of the heavens.

Let the higher levels of Trust begin.

75084589R00104

Made in the USA
Middletown, DE
02 June 2018